Elmer Lynnde

The Model Cook;

Things Good to Eat and How to Make Them

Elmer Lynnde

The Model Cook;
Things Good to Eat and How to Make Them

ISBN/EAN: 9783744782920

Printed in Europe, USA, Canada, Australia, Japan

Cover: Foto ©Andreas Hilbeck / pixelio.de

More available books at **www.hansebooks.com**

THE MODEL COOK;

OR,

Things Good to Eat and How to Make Them.

BY

ELMER LYNNDE.

NEW YORK:

O. JUDD CO., DAVID W. JUDD, Pres't,

751 BROADWAY.

1885.

To

My Daughter,

and the other Little Girls of the Land,
with the wish that they may grow up to be
Accomplished Housekeepers,
This Book is
Dedicated.

PREFACE.

It would seem as though a new cook book could hardly find a place in the world when the number of those already afloat is legion. Among them are the good, bad and indifferent; some very elaborately embellished, and produced quite regardless of expense, both in the style of the book and in the costly materials of the various dishes advocated, while others are poor and plain in every respect. This book does not profess to be elaborate, but its aim is to provide desirable as well as choice recipes, both for the table of the farmers and that of the merchants, and to keep it in a condensed form. To do this, I have avoided a great deal of useless repetition. For instance, I have not mentioned the manner of boiling or roasting every kind of meat, as the recipes that are given for two or three kinds will serve just as well for others. It is so in other departments of the book. I would add, however, that most of the recipes given are approved by some of the best housekeepers. May I hope that this little book will do its work, and be a comfort to the wives and mothers who are often puzzled to decide what to have for breakfast, dinner and tea for " Will " and the children.   ELMER LYNNDE.

(5)

THE MODEL COOK:

OR

Things Good to Eat, and How to Make Them.

SOUPS.

All will agree that soup is the necessary first course to a properly appointed dinner, and it is perhaps as well to make soups the first course in this practical receipt book. A variety of soups is given that will enable every one to find something to the taste.

As beef-tea or bouillon is now quite the thing for parties as well as for invalids, we head the list with that.

BEEF-TEA.

Have two pounds of beef off the round, chopped fine at the butchers', telling them that it is for beef-tea. Put it dry into a well-heated saucepan; stir it about five minutes, then add two pints of cold water, and when it comes to a boil, stir it twenty minutes; add salt and pepper, strain and serve for the table or for an invalid.

BEAN SOUP.—NO. I.

Boil your beans with a piece of salt pork. When thoroughly cooked, press the beans through a colander, after which, return them to the water, into which put four hard-boiled eggs, half a lemon sliced and a little pepper. Boil up and serve.

BEAN OR PEA SOUP.—NO. II.

Soak the beans, if dry, over night, and boil until soft. Press them through a colander. For each quart of liquid

(7)

allow one teaspoonful of sugar, one teaspoonful of salt, and a small saltspoonful of pepper. Add a beaten egg, a cup of milk, and two tablespoonfuls of butter. Some like to add a little lemon-juice on taking up. Canned sweet corn added is said to make good succotash for winter.

PARKER HOUSE SOUP.

Three quarts beef stock ; one carrot, one beet, one turnip, two small onions, all cut fine ; three quarts raw tomatoes, or one can of tomatoes. Boil all together one hour. Strain and mash through sieve. Put five ounces butter into a pan, heat to light brown ; stir into it five tablespoonfuls flour ; mix well, then add to the soup. Season with salt and pepper. Add one desertspoonful brown sugar. Set back on the fire to boil five minutes. Skim. Toast baker's bread, cut in small squares, put a few in each plate.

BEEF SOUP.

Three pounds of lean beef, with a marrow-bone ; a ham-bone, if you have it, or half-pound lean ham ; one turnip, one onion, one carrot, quarter of a cabbage, three stalks of celery, three quarts of cold water. Salt and pepper to taste. Cut the meat fine, and crack the bones. Put them in a pot with a close top, cover with one quart of water, and bring slowly to a boil ; the slower the better. When it begins to bubble, add the other two quarts of water, and boil slowly for three hours—two hours with closed top and the last with it slightly lifted. Wash and peel the turnip, carrot and onion ; scrape the celery and wash with the cabbage. Cut all into dice, and lay in cold water, slightly salted, for half an hour. Stew the carrot by itself in hot water until tender, then set aside to cool. Put the other vegetables on all together, in enough cold water to cover them, and let them boil to pieces. Strain them half an hour before taking up the soup, and press to a pulp. Return the liquid to the saucepan, throw in a little salt, and let it boil up once to clear it ; skim and add to the soup. Put in pepper and salt, unless the ham has salted it enough, and boil, covered, twenty minutes. Strain into an earthen dish ; let it get cold enough for the fat to rise. Skim off all you can. Rinse the pot with water ; return the soup to it; boil briskly one minute, and throw in the carrot. Skim and serve.

TURKEY SOUP.

Break up all the bones of one turkey ; add one pint soaked split peas, and three quarts of water. Put it on early in the morning ; add a little celery and salt for flavoring. Season with pepper and salt, and boil slowly until noon. Strain.

CLAM SOUP.—NO. I.

Boil about twenty-five clams, after washing them thoroughly in several waters, so as to remove the sand from the shells, until they open. Then take them off, chop the clams fine. Add the water in which they were boiled, with a piece of butter, a half tablespoonful of flour mixed thoroughly in a little milk and pepper. Let all come to a boil. They are also very nice stewed like oysters after boiling in their shells, without being chopped, but enough milk and butter and thickening added to make them rich.

CLAM SOUP.—NO. II.

Boil a knuckle of veal ; strain the liquor ; add twenty-five clams, chopped fine, four good sized potatoes, one onion ; drop dumplings. Season to taste with pepper, salt, sweet marjoram or parsley. Just before serving, thicken with one egg and flour, made smooth with a little cream.

SAGO SOUP.

Take good, clear, soup stock; remove the fat from the top and strain. Bring to a boil, and stir in half a cup of pearl sago, which has been well washed and soaked for half an hour in tepid water, or three hours in cold. Season if needed. Simmer half an hour, and pour out. Send around grated cheese with it.

MACARONI SOUP.

Take three pounds of beef. Add to it three quarts of water. Let it boil slowly over night. When cool the next day, skim off all the fat and pour off the liquid free from the sediment. About half an hour before dinner, set it on to boil, adding about a pint of macaroni broken up, and a tablespoonful and a half of stewed tomatoes or tomato catsup, salting it to the taste.

AMBER SOUP.

Take two pounds of soup-bone, a chicken, a small slice of ham, an onion, a sprig of parsley, half a small carrot, half a small parsnip, half a stick of celery, three cloves, pepper, salt, a gallon of cold water. Let the beef, chicken and ham boil slowly for five hours; add the vegetables and cloves to cook the last hour, having first fried the onion in a little hot fat, and then stick the cloves in it. Strain the soup into an earthen bowl, and let it remain over night. Next day remove the cake of fat from the top; take out the jelly, avoiding the sediment, and mix into it the beaten whites of two eggs with the shells. Boil quickly for half a minute, then, placing the kettle on the hearth, skim off carefully all the scum and white of the eggs from the top, not stirring the soup itself, which pass through the jelly bag, when it should be quite clear. The soup may then be set aside and reheated just before serving. Add then a large spoonful of caramel, as it gives a richer color and also a slight flavor.

TOMATO SOUP.

Boil slowly a knuckle of veal and beef-bone with celery. Strain and add part of a can of tomatoes. Cook half an hour, and strain again. Mix one tablespoonful of cracker powder with a cup of cream in a bowl. Add to it some of the soup, mix thoroughly and pour all back into the pot. Boil gently a few minutes and serve.

CHICKEN SOUP.

Cut the fowl into small pieces and lay in salt water for a half hour; place it in a soup kettle with three and one-half quarts of water; season with pepper and one onion. When the fowl is tender remove it, and add to the soup two well-beaten eggs, a cup of milk, and a dozen butter crackers.

OX-TAIL SOUP.

One ox-tail, two pounds lean beef, four carrots, three onions, thyme; cut the tail into several pieces and fry brown in butter. Slice the onions and two carrots, and after removing the ox-tail, put in these and brown also; when done, tie in a bag with a bunch of thyme and drop into the soup pot; lay the pieces of ox-tail in, then the meat in small pieces; grate over them the two whole carrots and add four quarts of cold water, with pepper and salt; boil from four to six hours, according to size of tail; strain fifteen minutes before serving and thicken with two tablespoonfuls of browned flour. Boil ten minutes longer.

DUMPLINGS FOR SOUP.

Half cup of sweet milk, one teaspoonful of cream tartar, half teaspoonful soda, a little salt, flour. Roll and cut, or mix thin enough to drop from a spoon.

FISH.

SALT CODFISH—BOILED.

Soak the fish over night, or seven or eight hours through the day. If wanted at noon, boil without soaking, changing the water several times, to remove the superfluous salt.

SALT CODFISH—BAKED.

Pick up the fish and freshen a little as for boiling; then place in a dish a layer of cracker crumbs, then one of fish; over each layer sprinkle pepper and butter until there are two layers of fish and three of crackers; then beat two eggs with milk enough to cover the whole, and bake about three-quarters of an hour.

FISH CHOWDER.

Take a good haddock, cod, or any other solid fish; cut it in pieces three inches square; put one pound of salt pork, cut in strips, into the pot, and fry it awhile; then take out the pork, put in a layer of fish, over that a layer of onions, sliced, then a layer of fish, with strips of the pork, and so on alternately, until the fish is all used. Mix some flour with water and season with pepper and salt to your taste, and add also a quart of sliced potatoes. Boil the whole three-quarters of an hour. Have ready some army crackers or pilot bread, throw them into the chowder, and serve.

CODFISH BALLS.—NO. I.

Pick up very fine, one quart of codfish; soak it in water over night; next morning put it in a saucepan. Slice thin as possible one quart of raw potatoes; put on top of the fish with enough cold water to cover them; cook until the potatoes are done; put in a colander and drain off all the water. Mix and add two eggs, a little pepper, and a lump of butter. Make into small balls, with the least possible flour, and drop into boiling lard.

CODFISH BALLS.—NO. II.

Take equal quantities of codfish and potatoes. Place the fish in cold water, over the fire, until tender; then drain and chop very fine. After the potatoes are boiled, mash very smooth. Add the fish, with a little milk, two beaten eggs and a tablespoonful of butter. Beat all well together; season with pepper; make into balls and fry in hot lard. Vary the proportion of fish and potatoes to suit the taste.

SALT CODFISH, WITH EGGS.

Pick the salt fish in small pieces; freshen with cold water, changing it two or three times. Put it in a saucepan with half a cup of boiling water, and a piece of butter the size of an egg, a little cayenne, and a round of onion, chopped finely. Stir smoothly one tablespoonful of corn starch in a little milk, add a cup of milk to the corn starch, pour it over the fish, and stir constantly until the butter melts and the whole is well cooked. Break two or three eggs into it. Serve hot.

SALT FISH—STEWED.

Tear a piece of fish into small strips, wash clean, soak in water for several hours, and place it in a basin with about a quart of water; let it simmer half an hour, then pour off the water and add one pint of new milk; when this comes to a boil, thicken with one teaspoonful of flour. Let it boil five minutes, then add butter the size of a walnut, and a little pepper, and serve.

BAKED SHAD.

Shad for baking should be carefully cleaned, but not split. Make a stuffing of bread crumbs, a little finely chopped pork, a suspicion of onion, some summer savory and chopped parsley and seasoning ; fill the fish and sew up. Put in a hot baking pan a slice of sweet salt pork, lay in the fish, and a couple of bay leaves, if at hand ; bake one hour, basting with its own juice.

BROILED SHAD.

Have the shad thoroughly cleaned, split it, and season well with salt and pepper. Lay the split side down upon a hot buttered gridiron, and when brown turn the fish. Serve on a hot dish with a good-sized piece of butter. Garnish with parsley and lemon.

CURRIED COD, HADDOCK OR SALMON.

Divide the fish into pieces about the size of a walnut, and then stew them in a sauce made as follows: To some sliced onion, fried slightly yellow in about an ounce of butter, add two tablespoonfuls of curry powder and a little flour, and then mix well with this about a pint of hot strong broth, made rather salt. When the fish has stewed in this sauce until cooked, the superfluous oil must be poured off, and the fish served with boiled rice ; a seasoning of lemon juice, may, if liked, be added to the sauce immediately before serving.

BOILED ROCK FISH.

After preparing the fish thoroughly, by drawing it and removing the scales, eyes, and gills, and then washing it, wrap it in a well-floured cloth ; put it into boiling water, well salted. It requires cooking about twenty minutes.

MEATS.

TO BOIL A HAM.

Wash the ham thoroughly in two or three waters, then put it on in boiling water and let it boil several hours, allowing about twenty or twenty-five minutes to a pound. When done, unless needed for immediate use, set it away and when cold skin it. On sending it to the table, put fringed letter paper around the shank. If preferred, glaze the ham by covering it with the beaten yolk of an egg, and then scattering pounded bread crumbs or cracker crumbs thickly over it, and set it in the oven a few minutes to brown. The large platter, on which it is served, looks well garnished with parsley.

BEEF TONGUE.

This is cooked in the same manner as the ham, allowing the same time to the pound. It is unnecessary to soak it over night, unless it is an exceptionally tough one. After boiling, skin it and slice it very thin, to send to the table. Garnish with parsley.

SAUSAGE MEAT.

Chop the pork, fat and lean together, very fine; season to taste, but be careful to use very little sage, as that spoils it for many persons. When thoroughly mixed put it in tin pails and pour melted lard over it to preserve it.

ROAST BEEF.

Wash the beef, season with salt and pepper and lay it in a dripping pan with about a cupful of water, and set in a good oven. Baste it, with its own gravy, a number of times. If it is required rare, about two hours will be long enough to cook it. Just before it is done, dredge it with flour to brown it. On taking it up, skim off the fat from the gravy, add a little flour and let boil up once or twice.

BAKED BEEF AND YORKSHIRE PUDDING.

After salting a fine rib, put it in the oven on bars made to fit the dripping pan. Pour a cup of water into the pan and when the meat is about half done add the pudding, made as follows : Beat four eggs very light, whites and yolks separate ; stir a pint of milk into the yolks and as much flour as will make a thin batter ; add a teaspoonful of salt, and lastly the whites. Take out the meat, pour the batter into the dripping pan, and then replace the meat and cook until the pudding is done. When dishing the meat, cut the pudding into squares and place them around it.

CORNED BEEF.

Wash the beef in several waters to remove the surplus salt. Set it on the fire in cold water, and let it come to a boil in about half an hour. Turn the meat several times, that every part may be cooked, and let it boil about three hours, if it is a medium-sized piece. When done, lay it on a dish and cover it with another, on which place a flatiron to press it. The pressing serves to extract the water and to make it firmer to slice.

BEEFSTEAK.—BROILED.

Take a tenderloin or sirloin beefsteak, and unless very tender, pound it with the back of a carving knife, which is better than a potato masher. Have the gridiron hot, and broil quickly, turning it constantly. When done place it on a hot dish, lay pieces of butter on it and season well with pepper and salt.

BEEFSTEAK.—FRIED.

Although epicures would scorn to eat a beefsteak if known to be fried, yet if it were done strictly according to directions we doubt if they would be able to detect the difference. Prepare the steak in the same way as for broiling. Have the frying-pan exceedingly hot ; just before putting the steak in, drop into it a piece of butter half the size of an egg. Turn the beefsteak constantly, and on taking it up season with pepper and salt. Keep it hot while dredging the frying pan, into which you have put a little hot water, with flour. Stir and boil this gravy a minute or two, and pour it over the steak. While the steak is cooking, be sure to keep the frying-pan covered.

A LEG OF MUTTON.

It may be either boiled or roasted. It should be put into hot water well salted, to boil, and you can ascertain when it is tender by trying it with a fork. The scum must be removed by frequent skimming. Serve with drawn butter. Roast it the same as you would veal, only not so long.

SHOULDER OF MUTTON.

A shoulder can be prepared for stuffing. For this, use stale bread crumbs seasoned with salt, pepper and thyme. If preferred add sage and onion.

MUTTON CHOPS.

Mutton chops should be cooked thoroughly but not allowed to burn. It is a good plan to parboil them, drain well, and then fry them in hot butter. The French chops are the more dainty and elegant for the table. In these, all the meat and fat at the narrow end of the chops are removed from the bone.

ROAST VEAL.

Season with pepper and salt, flour it and put it into a moderate oven. Baste at first with salt and water, afterward with the gravy. It requires a long time to cook, probably four hours for a piece of six or seven pounds. After removing it dredge the gravy with flour. Let it boil up, and serve.

VEAL CUTLETS.—FRIED.

Dip the cutlets in beaten egg, then into cracker or bread crumbs. Have the frying-pan hot and add a good-sized piece of butter before putting in the meat. Turn again and again until well done.

VEAL CUTLETS, A LA MILANAISE.

Brown some tender cutlets in boiling lard. Remove
them from the pan, and put enough flour into the lard
to thicken it; stir it thoroughly and when the flour
browns, add water enough to make the gravy about as
thick as cream. Fry a little onion, minced very fine, in
butter and add it to the gravy. Then put the veal
cutlets in and place round them about six sliced tomatoes.
Season; simmer gently about two hours, or until the
cutlets are tender.

VEAL PIE.

Line a deep tin pan with a good crust; parboil the
meat, and put it in; season high; nearly fill the pan with
water in which the meat was parboiled. Sprinkle flour
over, add a piece of butter, and cover with a tolerably
thick crust. Chicken, clam or oyster pie may be made
in the same manner. Oysters must not be cooked before
putting into the pie.

TURKEY OR CHICKEN.

TO ROAST.

After thoroughly drawing the fowls, add a piece of
baking soda, about the size of a pea, to the last water,
with which rinse thoroughly. Singe the hairs from the
fowls, using a lighted paper, and they will be ready
for stuffing. Use bread crumbs, salt, pepper, thyme,
and sage, and onion if desired, and then sew up the
opening with a coarse needle and thread. Lay the fowl
in a pan with about a cupful of water. Dredge with
flour before roasting and baste often. Allow about
fifteen minutes to the pound.

BONED CHICKEN.

Boil a chicken in a little soup stock until the bones
can be easily separated from the meat; remove all the

skin ; slice ; season with salt and pepper ; boil down the juice, pour it upon the meat, and shape it like a loaf of bread; wrap lightly in a cloth ; press it with a heavy weight for a few hours. When served, cut in thin slices.

FRICASSEED CHICKEN.

Wash the chicken thoroughly and cut up ; put into a pot and cover with cold water. Let it stew until tender. When done, have ready a thickening of cream or milk and flour, and stir it into the stew ; add butter, pepper, and salt. In the meantime have a nice shortcake, rolled as thin as pie-crust, baked and cut into squares. Lay the cakes on a large platter, and pour the chicken and gravy over them.

JELLIED CHICKEN.

Take an old fowl, cut in pieces, boil in a little more than a quart of water, with salt and pepper, until well done. Then take out the meat, cut it from the bones, skin it well and take off the fat. Return the bones and skin to the liquor and boil twenty minutes. Then strain through a cloth and set aside to cool. Cut the chicken into small bits ; place in a mould, sprinkling grated lemon over it, adding the juice. When the liquor is so cold that the fat can be removed, turn it carefully into the mould over the prepared chicken, not allowing any sediment to mingle with it. Set aside until the next day, then turn out and cut in thin slices. It is very nice for a supper dish.

CHICKEN PIE.

Take a pair of good young chickens, cut them in small pieces, adding a proper quantity of pepper and salt, and small strips of salt pork, and put the whole into a saucepan and cover with water. Boil for half an hour, add flour and butter to thicken the gravy. Provide a large dish for baking it, lined with paste ; put the contents of the sauce-pan into the dish, and cover with a good, rich paste, and bake the pie half an hour. It is best while fresh from the oven.

CROQUETTES.

CHICKEN CROQUETTES.

To one chicken, chopped, add a little salt, parsley, pepper, nutmeg, a saltspoon of onion, chopped fine, one cup of cream, one-quarter cup of butter, and one dessertspoonful of flour. Put the chicken, seasoning and cream on the fire; when hot stir in the butter and flour; cook about five minutes. When cold make into balls. Beat up an egg with bread crumbs, dip the balls in, and drop into boiling lard. Veal may be prepared in the same way.

CHICKEN CROQUETTES.—NO. II.

One large chicken, four sweet-breads, one-third of a common-sized loaf of bread, yolks of two eggs, half-pint of cream, parsley, nutmeg, pepper and salt. Take half a pint of the hot liquor in which the chicken was boiled, to which add the bread, leaving out the crust; chop the chicken very fine, parboil the sweet-breads, and chop fine, then stir them into the hot liquor, adding the eggs, cream and seasoning, and set away to cool. Mould, drop in beaten egg; roll in dry bread crumbs and fry like oysters.

VEAL CROQUETTES.

Two pounds of veal, one onion and a half, parsley, thyme, sage, pepper, salt, butter, and four eggs. Boil and chop the veal very fine; keep some of the liquor in which it is cooked. Chop the onions, and fry in butter until very soft. Then having the yolks of the eggs well beaten, and the seasoning, mix these with the meat and onions ; add the whites and the liquor to the rest ; mould and dip in bread crumbs and fry a light brown.

LOBSTER CROQUETTES.

To the meat of a well-boiled lobster, chopped fine, add pepper, salt, and powdered mace. Mix with this one-quarter as much bread crumbs, rubbed fine, as you have meat ; make into ovates, or pointed balls, with two table-spoonfuls of melted butter. Roll these in beaten egg, then in pulverized cracker, and fry in butter or very nice sweet lard. Serve dry and hot, and garnish with crisped parsley. This is a delicious supper dish or *entrée* at dinner.

RICE CROQUETTES.

These, seasoned with grated lemon-peel, are among the delicate dishes that take the place of heavy meats in summer. They look brown and taste crisp, and the color has considerable to do with making a table look inviting at this or any other season. Mould the rice in a wine-glass (it can be boiled with milk or plain, in water, as preferred), roll in bread crumbs and the yolk of an egg, and again in the crumbs, and fry lightly. You can add the white of the egg to the croquettes before moulding if you like.

SALMON CROQUETTES.

To a one pound can of salmon, chopped fine, add one teaspoonful of chopped parsley, piece of half a lemon, and a dust of cayenne. Mix thoroughly. Set a cup of cream on to boil. Rub one tablespoonful of butter and two tablespoonfuls of flour together until smooth, and stir them into the boiling cream, and let cook two minutes. Stir it into the salmon ; mix well ; turn out on a dish to cool. Form into croquette shapes with a wine-glass, roll in beaten egg and then in bread crumbs, and fry in olive-oil or butter ; drain on a piece of brown paper until not a particle of fat adheres. Serve on a napkin with parsley garnish.

OYSTER CROQUETTES.

After draining fifty oysters in a colander, chop them very fine. Strain the juice, and boil it down one-half; then add to it half a pound of butter, mixed very smoothly with a dessertspoonful of flour, and stir until it becomes a thickish smooth sauce; then add a teaspoonful of minced parsley, thyme, and half a teaspoonful of sweet marjoram. Now add the chopped oysters, a gill of rich cream, two or three beaten eggs, and a salt-spoon of salt. Stir these all well together to a thick paste. When it drops from the spoon in clumps it is done enough. Then pour it out on a large dish, spread it out and set it in a cool place to become stiff and cold, after which form the paste, with a little flour, to prevent it sticking to the hands, into small pear-shaped cones. When they are all done, dip each one separately into eggs beaten with a little of the oyster juice or milk, then roll in fine bread crumbs. When this coat of egg and crumbs is dry, give them a second coating, and fry in boiling lard until they are a delicate brown color.

CROQUETTES OF CHICKEN AND RICE.

Take one small chicken, boil and chop fine; then take the same quantity of boiled rice; mix well together and while hot add one beaten egg. When cold roll in beaten egg and crumbs, and fry in hot lard or butter.

RELISHES OF FISH, MEAT, ETC.

FISH CROQUETTES.

Take the remainder of cold, boiled fish, and after removing the bones, chop it fine with bread crumbs, and if convenient, a little cooked ham. Season with pepper and salt, and roll into balls. Dip in egg and bread crumbs or powdered crackers, and fry in hot lard.

VEAL HASH.

Into a cup of boiling water in a saucepan, stir a teaspoonful of flour, first wetting it with a spoonful of cold water, and let it boil about five minutes. Chop the veal very fine, with half as much stale bread. Put it in a pan and pour the gravy over it, letting it heat thoroughly, but not cook, for ten minutes. Have bread toasted and cut into delicate pieces and laid on the dish. Then place a large spoonful of hash on each piece of toast, and send it to the table very hot. Mutton and beef hash may be made in the same way.

MUTTON STEW.

A good mutton stew can be made by cutting the mutton into pieces about two inches square, and boiling them for two hours. Add of potatoes cut into quarters about as much as there is meat, seasoning with a little onion, pepper and salt. Finally add a thickening of flour mixed in a little milk.

MUTTON OR BEEF SCRAPS.

Chop the meat fine and put it into a saucepan with a cup of gravy, or of soup stock. Season with pepper and salt, and scatter over it, stirring all the time, a tablespoonful of flour. Let the meat heat gradually, and when boiling hot, set the pan on the back part of the range and poach some eggs to serve with the meat. When the eggs are done, put the meat on a platter and lay the eggs around the edge.

BITS OF STEAK.

The bits of sirloin steak that are left can be used to make an excellently flavored soup stock. Cut them into small pieces, and cook them slowly, with cold water enough to just cover them at first, then add boiling water and salt. To make a plain soup from them, add enough water to make a quart; to this allow a tablespoonful of tomato catsup, and a little browned flour mixed with the yolk of an egg ; a little onion and carrot chopped fine improve this for some tastes. Another way to use these pieces is to separate the fat from the lean ; save the fat to fry potatoes in, and chop the lean and make meat balls of it ; dip them into beaten egg and in fine cracker or bread crumbs, and use some of the fat to fry them in.

COLD ROAST BEEF, BROILED.

Cut a slice about a quarter of an inch thick from the undone part of the meat ; strew salt and pepper over it and place on the gridiron and heat it quickly ; turn it over four times in as many minutes and serve it upon a hot dish in melted butter ; it must be put to broil when the dinner-bell rings and served the moment it is to be eaten ; it will then be found very nice.

BEEF KIDNEY.

Lay it in salted water for half hour ; remove the white part as nearly as possible ; put the kidney in a stew-pan, cover with fresh water, and let it boil gently for six hours. Set it aside until needed. Chop very fine ; put it in a pan with a good piece of butter, a little of the water it was boiled in, pepper and salt ; if desired, a little flour to thicken it, or it may be poured over toast.

BEEF BALL.

One round of steak, two slices of fresh bread, three eggs, salt. Hash the meat with the bread, as fine as possible ; stir in the eggs and a little melted butter. Make into a loaf ; put into a dish with a little water in the bottom, and bake slowly one hour. Slice cold for supper. A little pork in it is good.

VEAL LOAF.

Three and a half pounds of fine-chopped veal ; seven crackers, pounded fine ; two eggs and the white of a third; butter the size of an egg, melted ; one tablespoonful of salt, one teaspoonful pepper, two tablespoonfuls sage, two slices of pork chopped. Knead well, and form into a loaf. Rub the outside with the yolk of an egg. Sift over it some powdered cracker. Lay on bits of butter. Baste with water, and bake two hours.

VEAL COLLOPS.

Parboil some sweet-breads, then dry on a coarse towel; cut them in pieces the size of an oyster; rub a seasoning of salt and pepper over each piece, dip in egg and cracker dust, and fry like doughnuts.

COLD PINK.

Take cold chicken or turkey, chop fine; stew cranberries, sweeten to the taste, and squeeze the juice, while boiling, over the turkey or chicken. Mix up well, put in a mould to form.

FRENCH STEW.

Grease the bottom of an iron kettle, and put into it three pounds of beef. Watch carefully that it does not burn, and turn it until it is brown all over. Then set a muffin-ring under the beef, to prevent its sticking; add a few sliced carrots, an onion sliced, and a cupful of hot water; cover closely and stew slowly until the vegetables are tender. Then add pepper and salt; serve on a dish with the vegetables. If more gravy is needed, add more hot water and thicken with flour.

CATSUPS, SAUCES, SALADS, ETC.

" Always have lobster sauce with salmon,
  And put mint sauce your roasted lamb on.
  Egg sauce—few make it right, alas !—
  Is good with bluefish or with bass.
  Nice oyster sauce gives zest to cod—
  A fish, when fresh, to feast a god."

SAUCE FOR SALAD OR FISH.

The yolks of two eggs boiled hard and mashed with a mustard-spoonful of mustard, black pepper, salt, three tablespoonfuls of salad-oil, and the same of vinegar. To some a tablespoonful of catsup would be an agreeable addition.

DRAWN BUTTER.

Rub a quarter of a pound of butter with a tablespoonful of flour; then add half a pint of water. Set on to boil; when done, add a hard-boiled egg cut into small pieces.

WHITE SAUCE.—FOR FISH, BOILED MUTTON, ETC.

Boil a large spoonful of flour, or grated potato, in enough water to make it the thickness of hot custard or very thin gruel. Add salt, pepper and grated nutmeg. When the potato is cooked, add a good piece of butter, which should merely melt in the sauce. At the moment of serving, add a small quantity of vinegar or a little lemon-juice. When the meat is on the platter, pour enough of the sauce over it to cover it, and let a little border of it lie all around it on the dish. Serve the remainder, if any, in a sauce-boat. Add a scant teaspoonful of capers just before serving.

CUCUMBER SAUCE.

Three dozen cucumbers, six or eight white onions, half pint salt, two quarts cider vinegar, quarter cup black pepper, one cup black mustard seed, six dozen cloves. Slice the cucumbers and onions, and put them with the salt in a bag to drain for six hours; then add pepper, mustard seed and cloves, and cold cider vinegar.

RELISH OF CABBAGE.

One good, crisp head of cabbage, shaved fine as possible; one tablespoonful of grated horseradish to each quart of cabbage; one pint cider vinegar; let come to a boil. Three eggs, a little salt. Beat the eggs well, stir into the vinegar until cooked, then pour it over the cabbage and set away to be eaten cold. It will keep several days.

CABBAGE SALAD.

One head of fine, white cabbage, minced small, three hard-boiled eggs, two tablespoonfuls of white sugar, one teaspoonful salt, one teaspoonful pepper, one teaspoonful made mustard, one teacupful of vinegar. Mix and pour upon the chopped cabbage.

COLD-SLAW OR CABBAGE SALAD.

Beat the yolks of four eggs to a very light cream ; then stir in gradually five tablespoonfuls of cider vinegar. Add two or three tablespoonfuls of sugar, and stir the mixture over the fire until it begins to thicken like boiled custard ; then remove and add a teaspoonful of butter and nearly a teaspoonful of anchovy mustard. Set the sauce upon ice to become cold, and pour it over the sliced cabbage just before serving. Celery is often mixed with the cabbage for this salad.

DRESSING FOR CABBAGE.—NO. II.

One egg, half cup of milk, half or two-thirds of a gill of vinegar, a little sugar. Beat up the egg with the milk, pour on the vinegar boiling hot, cook it with a little sugar, and set aside to cool. Shred the cabbage, season with pepper and salt, and pour over it the cold dressing.

CHICKEN SALAD.—NO. I.

Two large chickens, celery, one-half the quantity. Boil the chickens very tender, cut the celery and mix with it. Salad Dressing.—Eight eggs beaten to a froth, one pint of vinegar, four large tablespoonfuls of salad oil or melted butter, one large tablespoonful mixed mustard, one large tablespoonful salt, one teaspoonful of black pepper. Stir the whole together over a moderate fire constantly until sufficiently thick. When cold mix with the chicken and celery.

CHICKEN SALAD.—NO. II.

Ten pounds chicken, boiled, cut coarse, six stalks white celery, cut fine. *Dressing.*—Six eggs, hard-boiled, four tablespoonfuls olive oil, four tablespoonfuls of mixed mustard, half a pound of melted butter, half a cup of vinegar, quarter teaspoonful of red pepper, black pepper and salt to taste.

SALAD DRESSING.

Yolks of eight eggs, one tablespoonful of salt, three tablespoonfuls of prepared mustard, one tablespoonful of sugar, one cup of cream or milk, one cup of butter, cayenne pepper to taste. Stir well together over the fire, until it thickens like boiled custard, then add gradually one pint of vinegar.

SALAD DRESSING.—NO. II.

Yolks of six eggs, four tablespoonfuls salad oil, two tablespoonfuls mustard, two tablespoonfuls salt, three tablespoonfuls sugar. Boil the eggs thirty minutes and mix the yolks with the oil until they are entirely smooth; then add the other ingredients, and gradually enough vinegar to thin the mixture to suit the taste.

MAYONNAISE SAUCE OR SALAD DRESSING.

Rub the yolks of two raw eggs to a smooth paste, with half a teaspoonful of table salt, half a saltspoonful of cayenne pepper, a saltspoonful of dry mustard, and a teaspoonful of oil, or a teaspoonful and a half of melted butter. To this, when ready to serve the salad on which it is to be used, add vinegar and a little more oil, or in place of vinegar use strained lemon-juice; for ordinary purposes, good vinegar is just as satisfactory, and is, of course, much more economical.

COLD-SLAW.

Cut the cabbage and chop it, set a cup of cream or rich milk, over the fire, and when near boiling add a small cup of vinegar, pepper and salt. When it boils, draw it aside, and add a well-beaten egg ; pour hot over the cabbage and stir thoroughly.

CELERY SAUCE FOR BOILED FOWLS.

Wash the stalks, and cut them into thin slices about two inches long. Stew them until tender in a little weak gravy or water. Season with powdered mace, pepper and salt ; then add the juice of a lemon, and thicken with a small piece of butter which has been kneaded in flour.

POTATO SALAD.

Boil very carefully from six to eight medium-sized potatoes ; let them get cold, then slice them thin ; two silver-skin onions minced very fine, so as to get the flavor and not detect the pieces of onion ; mix the latter with the parsley and the potatoes ; season with salt and cayenne pepper. Take one-third of a teaspoonful of dry mustard, moisten it with a teaspoonful of water, add the yolks of two eggs; beat together with an egg-beater until well mixed, then drop in salad oil, beating it all the time until it thickens like a custard, then add one and a half tablespoonfuls of vinegar. Pour the dressing over the potatoes, and mix all together. The dish may be garnished with salad leaves or celery tops.

TOMATO CATSUP.

Half a bushel of tomatoes, six onions, half a pound of sugar, one pound of salt, quarter pound of ground mustard, two ounces ground cloves, two ounces black pepper, quarter ounce cayenne pepper, a handful of peach leaves. Boil all together two hours, or longer if the tomatoes are very watery, and just before taking from the fire add one quart of cider vinegar. If it boils after the vinegar is

added it will turn dark. Pour through colander; bottle
and seal.

TOMATO SOY.—NO. I.

Nine ripe tomatoes, peeled and chopped; two bell
peppers, seeds and cores removed; one onion chopped
with the pepper; two cups of vinegar, one tablespoonful
of salt, two tablespoonfuls of sugar, one teaspoonful each
of ginger, allspice and cloves.

TOMATO SOY.—NO. II.

One peck of ripe tomatoes, peeled; one quart of vinegar, three and one-half pounds of dark brown sugar;
one ounce of whole cloves. Boil together very slowly
until it is thick, and reduced fully two-thirds. This will
keep for years, and is good with poultry, game, etc.

PICKLES.

TOMATO PICKLES.

One peck of green tomatoes, six peppers, four onions
with one cup of salt sprinkled through them, and allowed
to stand one night. In the morning pour off the water.
Boil in a kettle, with vinegar enough to cover them, and
one cup of sugar, one tablespoonful of cloves, one tablespoonful each of allspice, cinnamon, and horseradish,
until quite soft. Pack in stone jars.

FRENCH PICKLES.—NO. I.

Half a peck of green tomatoes, two heads of cabbage,
half a dozen peppers, one cup of brown sugar, half an
ounce of mustard (whole), allspice (whole), and celery-
seed. Salt over night; squeeze out the water in the
morning; cover with vinegar (it takes about two quarts),
and boil about one hour.

FRENCH PICKLES.—NO. II.

Slice half a peck of green tomatoes ; lay them in salt over night ; in the morning squeeze the tomatoes dry ; add twelve sliced onions, whole allspice and cloves ; dust with pepper ; cover with cider vinegar ; simmer six hours.

FRENCH PICKLES.—NO. III.

One peck of green tomatoes, half a peck of string beans, a quarter peck of white onions, one pint of small red peppers, two large heads of white cabbage, one pound of brown sugar, one box of ground mustard, two table-spoonfuls of celery-seed, two tablespoonfuls each of whole cloves and allspice. Slice the tomatoes, making a layer of tomatoes and a sprinkling of salt till all are done. Let them stand over night. In the morning press the water from them. Cut the cabbage as for slaw. Slice the onions ; cut up the beans and thoroughly mix all together. Boil two hours in a preserving-kettle, with vinegar to cover.

CHOW-CHOW.

Two large heads of cabbage, half a peck of green tomatoes, eighteen peppers, ten cucumbers, eight onions, three tablespoonfuls dry mustard, two tablespoonfuls brown sugar, and two of celery-seed. Chop, and salt down over night. Pour off the water, and cover with cider vinegar.

———

OYSTERS AND CLAMS.

OYSTERS WITH TOAST.

Butter a few slices of toast, lay on a shallow dish ; heat the liquor of the oysters ; season, and just before it boils, add the oysters ; let them boil up once, then pour them over the toast.

FRICASSEED OYSTERS.

Fifty oysters, six ounces of butter, three tablespoonfuls of flour, three saltspoonfuls of salt, two each of whole pepper and mace, one quart of cream, four yolks of eggs, one teacupful of bread crumbs. Set the oysters, with their juice, in a stew-pan on a quick fire; give one boil, drain them, put them into a hot tureen and set in a warm place. Rub the butter, flour and three tablespoonfuls of scalding cream to a fine, smooth paste; stir it quickly into the quart of cream, on a quick fire; add the salt and spices and stir until it no longer thickens. Now add the yolks of the eggs, well beaten; stir until smooth, strain the whole through a fine sieve upon the oysters, cover evenly with the crumbs, and lightly brown in a quick oven.

STEWED OYSTERS.—NO. I.

" The Caterer " says that the following is the Philadelphia style of stewing oysters : Fifty oysters, four ounces butter, four tablespoonfuls cracker dust, two saltspoonfuls salt, one saltspoonful white pepper, one saltspoonful mace, two teaspoonfuls whole allspice, one pinch cayenne pepper. Put the oysters and their juice into a bright stew-pan, set on a quick fire, add the butter, salt and spices, sift in the cracker dust, stir gently till well mixed; at the first boil pour them into a hot tureen, cover and serve immediately. If cooked longer they shrivel, and get tough and indigestible.

STEWED OYSTERS.—NO. II.

Drain in a colander a pint of oysters from their liquor, letting them drain for five minutes. Remove the oyster liquor, and pour a pint of boiling water on the oysters, throwing this water away. Add a pint of fresh boiling water to the oyster liquor, and let it boil in a saucepan, until all the scum that rises has been skimmed off; then add a pint of fresh milk, one powdered water cracker, a piece of butter, salt and pepper. Boil ten minutes and just before the soup is to be served, turn in the oysters from the colander and let them scald for three minutes. Oyster soup prepared in this way will not disagree with invalids.

PANNED OYSTERS.

Take a dozen fresh, large oysters such as are used for frying. Have ready a frying-pan with a handle to it, into which put the oysters with their own liquor, and that of a dozen others. In this dish there is no water and no milk, nothing but oyster juice, pure and simple. Add one ounce of butter, a little black pepper, and a pinch of salt. Sprinkle on the top a small quantity of cracker dust. Place on a quick fire. When the oysters begin to swell they are done, requiring only five minutes to cook. Eat them directly from the pan while they are steaming hot.

ROASTED OYSTERS.

Select large, fresh oysters. Having washed their shells thoroughly, place them in a dripping-pan with the round shell down. Set them in a hot oven for about twenty minutes. Serve in the shells.

SCALLOPED OYSTERS.

Have a scallop shell, or pudding dish, into which put a layer of bread crumbs and butter, then a layer of oysters, seasoning each layer with pepper and salt. To the third layer of oysters add a little butter and the juice of the oysters. Place the dish in an oven for about twenty minutes, or until brown on top.

TO PREPARE OYSTERS FOR PATTIES.

Set the oysters in a stew-pan on the fire, in their own liquor, and when they begin to simmer, skim them out quickly. Pour out all liquor, except what is necessary for making a sauce ; skim this well and make as thick as rich cream, with flour and butter smoothed together. Season well with salt and cayenne pepper ; add a little nutmeg, if liked ; when cooked enough, take the sauce off of the fire, add the yolks of two or three eggs, well beaten, and the oysters. Let them merely become hot again, without boiling ; fill the pastry and serve immediately.

OYSTER PIE.

Take one hundred large oysters, drain them. Line a dish with a rich paste ; then put in a layer of oysters, seasoned with mace, pepper and salt ; add a lump of butter, the size of a nutmeg, and dust a little flour over them ; then add the liquor of the oysters, and dust a little flour over that. Add the top crust and bake one hour.

STEWED CLAMS.

Small clams are the best for stewing. Wash the shells thoroughly in several waters, to get rid of the adhering sand. Cover them with boiling water. When the shells open, take out the clams and put them in a saucepan with a small quantity of the liquor. Have ready some boiling milk in another pan, into which put a good-sized piece of butter. Add the clams, when both are just off the boil, and season with a little pepper. For a change, this is a good relish for breakfast.

ROAST CLAMS.

These are very nice if properly done. Select either large or small clams. Lay them on the coals, and as their shells open, watch them closely until they are somewhat cooked. Send them to the table as hot as possible, on the half shell, with a small piece of butter on each.

MINCED CLAMS.

Boil some clams in the shells until they open. Chop them fine, and mix some bread crumbs with them, a little butter and pepper. Fill the half shells with the mixture, and bake for a short time in the oven, having placed them in a large pan to keep them steady.

VEGETABLES.

BOILED POTATOES.

Pare the potatoes very thin. Throw them into cold water and let them stand for about half an hour. Then have ready boiling water, salted, and let the potatoes boil hard until tender, as shown by trying them with a fork. Pour off the water, and leave them in the pot on the corner of the range until dry. When potatoes are to be boiled in their skins, set them on range in cold water.

BAKED POTATOES.

Use large potatoes for baking, washing them thoroughly, and wiping them before placing them in the oven. Bake for about an hour, and serve on a dish with a napkin folded over them.

MASHED POTATOES.

Old potatoes are generally served as follows : After boiling and drying, mash them, adding butter and a little milk. Put them into a dish and work them into an oval shape with a knife ; cover with the yolk of an egg, well beaten, and brown in the oven. Another way of arranging them after adding the butter and milk, is to squeeze them through a colander on a platter and garnish with parsley. This makes a very pretty dish for high days and holidays.

STEWED POTATOES.

Slice cold boiled potatoes into a saucepan, add two ounces of butter, a dessertspoonful of flour, a wineglass-

ful of cream or milk, pepper and salt. Stew for a few
minutes.

SARATOGA POTATOES.

If the potatoes are to be eaten at breakfast, they should
be peeled the evening before and shaved into slices the
thickness of an old fashioned wafer, and left in water
over night ; in the morning drain them perfectly dry
from the water, and have ready a kettle of boiling lard,
into which drop a few pieces at a time ; when nicely
browned on one side, turn them, and when both sides
are brown, take them out with a skimmer and send them
to the table hot.

BROILED POTATOES WITH HAM.

Slice cold boiled potatoes in rather thick slices ; place
on a greased gridiron and broil brown ; mince some cold
boiled ham very fine, and a very little shalot, or onion
and parsley ; fry in butter until a light brown color ; dish
the potatoes neatly, and pour the ham, etc., on them.
Serve very hot. This is very nice for breakfast, with
coffee, boiled oatmeal, stewed prunes, and hominy croquettes.

SCALLOPED POTATOES.

Two cups of mashed potatoes, two tablespoonfuls of
cream or milk, and one of melted butter ; salt and pepper
to taste. Stir the potatoes, butter and cream together,
adding one raw egg. If the potatoes seem too moist,
beat in a few fine bread crumbs. Bake in a hot oven for
ten minutes, taking care to have the top a rich brown.
A nice dish for tea.

POTATO SCONES.

Mash any cold potatoes which may have been left from
a previous meal until quite smooth, adding a little salt
and flour. Mould into cakes of the required thickness,
and brown on a griddle. Eat with butter.

STUFFED POTATOES.

Bake large potatoes until thoroughly done ; cut an end off of each and scrape out the inside ; mash this with milk, butter, a couple of well-beaten eggs, a little salt and pepper. Fill the mixture into the skins, return the cap to each and set them in a large pan in the oven until they are exceedingly hot. Send them to the table in a dish wrapped in a napkin.

POTATO PUFF.

Add to cold mashed potato two or three well-beaten eggs, salt, butter the size of an egg, and cream or milk. Beat this together until very light ; have a pudding dish ready to receive it, and then bake in the oven to a light brown. It is also very nice baked in little patty-pans

SWEET POTATOES, BOILED.

Have the water boiling, into which drop the sweet potatoes with their skins on ; when they are tender, pour off the water, so as to drain them thoroughly, then peel them and set in the oven to dry.

SWEET POTATOES, BAKED.

Wash the potatoes and set them in a good, steady oven, with their skins on, of course.

TO KEEP SWEET POTATOES.

We know of an excellent housekeeper who buys all her sweet potatoes in the fall, before cold weather sets in, at which time they are apt to get frosted and spoiled. She wraps the potatoes separately in newspaper, and has excellent, mealy potatoes in winter, when others are eating those that are soggy and tasteless. Of course they must be kept in a dry, warm place.

CORN.

Some people boil corn in the husks, as they think it gains much in sweetness. This would do very well if there were no large worms hiding away in the green folds, but of course each ear would have to be thoroughly examined and then wash husks and all. However, young sweet corn is a very delightful vegetable, in the husks or out. It should be put into boiling salted water, and requires only twenty minutes, if young and tender.

BAKED GREEN CORN.

A novel way to serve green corn is the following : Grate one dozen ears of tender corn ; add one quart of sweet milk, in which has been stirred until free from lumps, three tablespoonfuls of flour, a quarter of a pound of butter, or a piece as large as an egg will do ; four eggs, whites and yolks beaten together, with pepper and salt to your taste. Butter a large earthen pudding dish and bake this mixture for one hour. To be served with meat and potatoes as a vegetable, though with the addition of sugar and with a rich sauce, it takes the place of a pudding.

SUCCOTASH.

Lima beans are best to use with corn for succotash, though other beans can be used. Cut the corn from the cob, but not too close. The beans will require about three-quarters of an hour to boil, and the corn only twenty minutes ; therefore set the beans on first, throwing in the corn cobs with them in order to save the sweetness of the corn, which is said to lie close to the cob. Before adding the corn, remove the cob from the beans ; then, after the corn has boiled twenty minutes, add a large cupful of milk, a teaspoonful of flour, wet up with cold milk, a large piece of butter, and pepper and salt to taste.

PORK AND BEANS.

Take two pounds of side pork, neither too fat nor too lean, and two quarts of navy beans. Soak the beans one night in a gallon of milk-warm water. After breakfast, scald and scrape the rind of the pork, and let it boil an hour, then add the beans ; as soon as they boil up, pour off the water, and put on a gallon of fresh water ; boil until the beans are tender, adding more boiling water if necessary ; put them into a bean pot ; first a slice of pork, then the beans with four tablespoonfuls of molasses, then the remainder of the pork with the rind uppermost, well scored ; season with pepper and salt if needed, and cover with the liquor left in the pot and hot water. Baking from four to six hours, or even longer will not injure them ; add hot water as needed, keep the cover on pot until an hour before serving, when it is to be removed, to allow the pork to brown.

TURNIPS, BOILED.

Boil turnips in a pot by themselves. When tender, mash them, add salt and butter, and if old, a little white sugar. In boiling, use plenty of water, which should be salted. Boil for about an hour.

ASPARAGUS.

Wash the asparagus thoroughly, then bind it together, that the stalks may not be cut, using a strip of muslin about an inch in width. Have the water boiling and salted, and boil about twenty minutes. Prepare some pieces of toast, lay them at the bottom of the dish, on which place the asparagus unbound, and pour drawn butter over it.

SPINACH.

Pick over the leaves carefully, wash thoroughly, boil in salted water for about twenty minutes. Drain it on a colander, chop it fine, and then heat the chopped spinach in a stew-pan with pepper, and butter the size of an egg. Stir it constantly, and when thoroughly hot, turn it out upon a dish and mould it with a spoon, smoothing the surface to bring it into a rounded form. Hard-boiled eggs cut into thin slices may be placed on top.

ONIONS.

After peeling the onions, throw them into cold water; let them remain a few minutes, then drop them into boiling water and boil until half done. Pour off the water, then put them into equal quantities of milk and water with salt. When done take them up, adding butter to a little of their gravy and pouring it over them.

BOILED CARROTS AND PARSNIPS.

The carrots must be split lengthwise, else the outside will be done before the inside is sufficiently cooked. Salt the water and boil about an hour, if the carrots are young, or two hours when old. Parsnips may be cooked in the same way.

GREEN PEAS.

After the peas are shelled, lay them in cold water; then put them into boiling salted water and cook fifteen or twenty minutes. Add a teaspoonful of white sugar, and when dished, a little butter.

EGG PLANT, BAKED.

Parboil the egg plant fruit until it is soft enough to stick a straw into it; then cut it just in half; scoop out the inside, leaving the shell; chop it up very fine, and season very highly with pepper and salt, a good deal of butter, and bread crumbs. Mix all well together and return it into the shell; then strew crumbs of bread on the top, and bake for an hour.

EGG PLANT, FRIED.

Peel the egg plants, slice them, sprinkle a little salt over the slices, pile them up, and let them remain half an hour; wipe the slices dry, dip them in beaten yolk of egg, then in grated cracker, and fry them a light brown in boiling lard, seasoning them slightly with pepper while they are cooking. Another way is to parboil the egg plants, after they are peeled, in water with a little salt, then slice thin, dust them with corn meal, flour, or corn starch, and fry them brown. After the egg plant is peeled and sliced, the slices should be placed one upon another and covered with a plate, on which is placed a flat-iron, to press out the juice which is not used.

BEETS, BAKED.

Wash the beets perfectly clean, place then in a pan, with very little water, and bake until they are tender. The time will, of course, vary with the size of the beet, an hour being small enough allowance for a beet of medium size. When they are tender, remove the skin and serve in the same way as boiled beets.

BEETS, BOILED.

Beets must be thoroughly washed, but not touched with a knife until after they are boiled, or they will lose their sweetness. Young beets require about an hour to boil; old ones three hours.

MACARONI WITH TOMATOES.

Cut up a quantity of tomatoes, and remove from each the seeds and watery substance it contains. Stew them in a saucepan, with a small piece of butter, pepper, salt and some thyme; add a few spoonfuls of either soup stock or gravy; keep stirring while on the fire, until they are reduced to a pulp; pass through a hair sieve, and dress the macaroni with the sauce thus obtained, and plenty of freshly grated cheese.

MACARONI WITH EGGS.

Break half a pound of macaroni into short bits, cook tender in boiling salted water; drain well, put into a deep dish, and pour over it a cupful of drawn butter, in which have been stirred two beaten eggs and two table-spoonfuls of grated cheese, with salt and pepper. Loosen the macaroni to allow the sauce to penetrate it, and mix more grated cheese with it. Place in the oven until the sauce thickens and the top is slightly brown.

MACARONI WITH OYSTERS.

Cook half a pound of macaroni until soft, in boiling salted water. Drain on a colander. Put a layer in a dish, season with pepper and salt, cover with little bits of butter, then a layer of oysters, and another of maraconi until the dish is full ; add one pint of hot milk. Grate some bread crumbs fine, mix with a well-beaten egg and spread over the top, Bake in a hot oven until brown.

MACARONI, BOILED.

Break about half a pound of pipe macaroni into small pieces. Throw it into boiling salted water, and after boiling twenty minutes take it out, and arrange it in a pudding dish, in layers, with grated cheese and butter the last layer being of macaroni, without any cheese or butter. Bake about an hour.

TOMATOES, SLICED.

When tomatoes first come, if they are fully ripe, they make a nice dish for tea, peeled, sliced, and laid in a green dish to set off the color, and covered with mayonnaise sauce.

TOMATOES, BAKED.

Slice the tomatoes into a pudding dish, sprinkling pepper and salt between the layers. Scatter small pieces of butter here and there, and grate crackers over the whole. Bake for about two hours.

TOMATOES, STEWED.

Pour boiling water over the tomatoes, cover closely for about ten minutes ; then peel and slice them, adding salt, pepper and butter. Stew until done, stirring frequently while stewing.

SCALLOPED TOMATOES.

Scald fully ripe tomatoes, remove the skins, cover the bottom of a buttered pudding dish with a layer of tomatoes seasoned with pepper and salt, cover with a layer of bread and butter, and so on, alternately, until the dish is full, finishing at the top with tomatoes. Bake in a moderate oven one-half hour, serve hot in the dish in which it was baked.

TOMATOES, STUFFED.

To prepare tomatoes in this way, the finer and larger they are the better. Remove a circular piece from the stem end. Take out the inside without breaking the skin. Mix the portion removed with bread crumbs, salt, pepper; grated corn, if at hand; a little butter and sugar. Fill up the skins with the mixture, cover the end again, place in a dish, and bake for about three quarters of an hour.

EGGS.

BOILED EGGS.

Seven minutes will boil eggs hard; boiled from two and one-half to three minutes, they will be soft.

FRIED EGGS.

Break each egg by itself and fry in a little butter. Fry only on one side, unless they are required to be hard. If ham is served with them, it is well to fry them in the ham fat instead of butter.

SCRAMBLED EGGS.

Six eggs, half a teacup of milk, salt, pepper and toast. Heat the eggs, milk and pepper in a frying-pan, and as the mixture begins to cook, scramble it up with a knife until thoroughly done. Have ready some small pieces of toast, on which to serve it.

OMELET.—NO. I.

Six eggs, one cup of sweet milk, three tablespoonfuls of flour, one tablespoonful of melted butter. Salt.

OMELET.—NO. II.

Four eggs, half a cup of milk or cream. Salt. Beat the yolks and whites separately, and stir in the whites just before baking.

OMELET.—NO. III.

Allow two tablespoonfuls of milk to each egg ; beat the yolks and whites separately ; add a little salt ; pour into a hot skillet, in which a piece of butter, the size of a walnut, has been melted. The skillet should be as hot as it can be without scorching the butter. As the omelet bubbles and rises, run a thin-bladed knife under it ; every now and then, that it may not burn ; cook two or three minutes, or until the eggs set ; fold over, shake the skillet, turn on a hot platter and serve at once.

OYSTER OMELET.

Eighteen or twenty large oysters, six eggs, one teaspoonful of corn-starch mixed in a little milk, butter the size of a large nutmeg, salt and pepper to taste. Chop the oysters very fine. Beat the yolks and whites of the eggs separately, and then together, and stir in the corn-starch and oysters. Melt in a frying-pan a piece of butter the size of a walnut, when this is boiling hot, pour in the omelet. Brown slowly, and serve on a hot dish.

VEAL OMELET.

Three and a half pounds of veal, chopped fine, eight tablespoonfuls of rolled crackers, one nutmeg, two eggs, three tablespoonfuls of cream, salt and pepper to the taste, a piece of butter the size of an egg. Bake in a batter-pan with cracker-dust, two hours.

DRIED BEEF OMELET.

Cover with water, in a frying-pan, one-quarter pound of sliced dried beef; when it boils, pour off the water. Chop the beef very fine in a wooden bowl. Beat six eggs very light, yolks and whites separate ; add the beef with a little pepper, and a small cupful of milk. Melt a piece of butter in the frying-pan, pour in the mixture and fry to a light brown, rolling up the edges with a knife until it is done.

ŒUFS DE LA CROQUEMITAINE.

Add to three tablespoonfuls of cream or milk, in a stew-pan, a little grated tongue or beef, pepper and salt. When quite hot, add four eggs, well beaten ; stir all the time until the mixture becomes quite thick. Have ready a couple of slices of bread, toasted and buttered. Spread the mixture on the toast and send it to the table very hot.

POACHED EGGS.

To present a nice appearance, poached eggs must be cooked with care. An egg-poacher may be used, but a broad pan filled with boiling water with muffin rings placed in it is more easily handled. Only the freshest eggs should be used. Open each egg into a saucer, and when all are ready, drop each one into a muffin ring. Two minutes' simmering will cook them sufficiently. Have ready a hot platter, with small pieces of boiled ham, or thin slices of well buttered toast. Take the eggs from the water with a draining ladle, and slip each one carefully on the toast. Sprinkle a very little salt and pepper upon each egg. Garnish the dish with bits of parsley.

HOMINY, OATMEAL AND RICE.

BOILED HOMINY.

Set a teacup of hominy over the fire in cold water, with a little salt. Boil for an hour, stirring frequently.

FRIED HOMINY.

Add to cold boiled hominy a piece of butter about half the size of an egg. Also a teacupful of cream, and enough flour, or white Indian meal, to stiffen it. Season with salt. Stir it up thoroughly; make into small cakes and fry in butter, on a griddle.

OATMEAL.

If wanted for a very early breakfast, soak the oatmeal over night, in a small quantity of water. In the morning, cook in a farina kettle, or in a common jar set in a vessel of water, for about half an hour. Cracked wheat may be cooked in the same manner.

RICE IN CHINESE STYLE.

The process of boiling one pound of rice is as follows : Take a clean stew-pan with a close-fitting top, and a clean piece of white muslin, large enough to cover over the top of the pan and hang down inside nearly to, but not in contact with the bottom. Into the sack so formed place the rice, pour over it two cupfuls of water, and put on the cover of the stew-pan so as to hold up the muslin bag inside, and fit tightly all round. Place the pan on a slow fire, and the steam generated from the water will cook the rice. Each grain, it is stated, will come out of the boiler as dry and distinct as if just taken from the hull. More water may be poured into the pan if necessary, but only sufficient to keep up the steam until the rice is cooked. The pan must not be heated so hot as to cause the steam to blow off the lid.

BREAD.

HOW TO MAKE YEAST.

A handful of hops, and a common-sized potato are to be boiled together, until the potato is done. Then take one teacupful of flour, and one good-sized teaspoonful each of ginger and of brown sugar. Stir the water in which the potato and hops were boiled with the other ingredients and set it aside until cool. Then add three tablespoonfuls of good baker's yeast. Let it stand until well risen, perhaps five or six hours, and keep it in the cellar. Use about two tablespoonfuls of this yeast in enough biscuit or muffins for one meal, and the same quantity for two good-sized loaves of bread.

YEAST.—NO. II.

One dozen potatoes, with one pint of hops, boiled in one gallon of water. Strain the liquor through a colander, and when cool, add one teacupful of sugar, one pint of baker's yeast, and salt. Let it rise one day ; then cover up close, and it will keep for a month.

TO MAKE LIGHT BREAD.

Knead the dough and set it to rise ; knead it again, and set it to rise, and so repeat the process several times.

BREAD.—NO. I.

Stir one cup of flour into one quart of boiling milk. When cool, add four potatoes, mashed fine, a little salt, a tablespoonful of sugar, one teacup of yeast, and enough flour to make a stiff sponge. Let it stand over night, and knead in the morning.

BREAD.—NO. II.

Pour one pint of boiling water upon one pint of flour. Set away until lukewarm ; add one and one-quarter cup of yeast, one quart of warm water, with flour enough to make a stiff batter. When risen, add a piece of lard the size of an egg, and flour enough to mould easily. Mould for ten minutes, put into pans, and let it rise until very light, then bake. Mrs. G.'s Recipe.

BREAD SPONGE.

Three pounds of flour, one ounce of compressed yeast, half a tablespoonful of salt, one pint and three gills of tepid water (two-thirds cold, one-third boiling). Place the flour in a large basin, and add salt; the yeast in another basin, and water in a pitcher. If the water is too hot, the bread will be full of holes; if too cold, the bread will be heavy. With half a gill of the water make the yeast perfectly smooth, and then, with the remainder of the water, pour it into the centre of the flour, stirring the flour from the sides. Stand the sponge in a warm place for about two hours, when it is ready for use. With baker's yeast, of course, it might stand all night. Miss Dod's Recipe.

GRAHAM BREAD.

One quart of water boiled (use warm), two large tablespoonfuls of yeast, a pinch of salt. Stir in flour enough to make a thin batter; let it rise over night; in the morning add half a cup of brown sugar, a pinch of soda, and stir in graham flour until it is a stiff batter. Let it rise again, and bake in a moderate oven.

BROWN BREAD.—NO. I.

One pint of buttermilk or sour milk, one cup of molasses, one teaspoonful of soda, graham flour sufficient to make a light batter. Mix the buttermilk and molasses together thoroughly. Add the flour and then the soda, which should be mixed with a little of the milk. Give the whole a thorough beating. Steam in a pan for two hours, afterward bake twenty minutes.

BROWN BREAD.—NO. II.

One pint and a half of bread sponge, half a teaspoonful of soda dissolved in water, four large tablespoonfuls molasses. Stir in graham flour until as thick as muffins. Let it rise until light, and bake.

BOSTON BROWN BREAD.

Four cups of rye meal (not flour), two cups of Indian meal, one cup of flour, one cup of molasses, one teaspoonful each of salt and of soda. Mix with cold water to a thick batter, and steam three or four hours.

DYSPEPSIA BREAD.

Three quarts of graham flour, one quart of warm water, one gill of molasses, one teaspoonful of soda, one gill of yeast; let it rise over night. Bake two hours.

CORN BREAD.—NO. I.

Three cups of yellow meal, two cups of flour, two eggs, one cup of sugar, three teaspoonfuls of cream of tartar, one teaspoonful and a half of soda, half a teaspoonful of salt. Mix with sweet milk. Bake in a quick oven.

CORN BREAD.—NO. II.

One cup and a half of sour cream, half a cup of white sugar, one egg, one teaspoonful of soda, one teaspoonful of salt. Add one-third white flour, two-thirds Indian meal, to make a stiff batter.

CORN BREAD.—NO. III.

Two eggs, one quart of milk, two pounds of Indian meal, two teaspoonfuls of Rumford yeast-powder. Stir all well together; bake in buttered pans.

CORN BREAD.—NO. IV.

Two cups of yellow meal, two cups of sweet milk, two eggs, two tablespoonfuls of sugar, a piece of butter the size of an egg, two teaspoonfuls of cream tartar, one teaspoonful of soda.

ANNIE'S CORN BREAD.—NO. V.

Two cups of Indian meal, two cups of flour, two and one-half cups of milk, half a cupful of white sugar, a pinch of salt, two tablespoonfuls of melted butter, three teaspoonfuls of baking powder.

NANTUCKET CORN CAKE.

Two small cups of white Indian meal, poured slowly into one quart of boiling milk. When cool, add six eggs, yolks and whites beaten separately, two table-spoonfuls of sugar, one teaspoonful of salt. Bake in rings or pans.

BISCUIT, ROLLS, ETC.

ROLLS.

Rub half a teacupful of butter into one pound of flour, add half a teacupful of yeast, a little salt, and sufficient warm milk to make a stiff dough. Cover and set it in a warm place that it may rise in two hours. Mould into biscuits lightly, and bake in fifteen minutes.

FRENCH ROLLS.

Two quarts of flour, one pint of milk, half a cupful of sugar, half a cupful of yeast, two tablespoonfuls of lard, one teaspoonful of salt. Rub the lard and salt into the flour. Scald the milk and let it cool to blood heat. Add sugar and yeast to the milk. Make a hole in the flour and pour the mixture into it without stirring. Do this at or before tea; then let it stand in a warm place until next morning. Knead thoroughly and let it rise again until afternoon. Then roll out in rounds, spread melted butter over them and double over. Let them rise in pans.

ASTOR HOUSE ROLLS.

Into two quarts of flour put a piece of butter the size of an egg, a little salt, one tablespoonful of white sugar, one pint of milk, scalded and added when warm ; half a cup of yeast, or one small cake. When the sponge is light, mould for fifteen minutes ; let rise again, roll out, cut into round cakes ; when light, flatten with the hand or rolling-pin, place a piece of butter on top, and fold each over upon itself. When light, bake in a quick oven.

PARKER HOUSE ROLLS.

A quart of milk and a tablespoonful of butter ; boil together ; one cup of yeast, a tablespoonful and a half of sugar ; flour enough to make a stiff batter. Set to rise until light. Knead, make into rolls, and let them rise one hour.

BREAD STEAKS.

Beat up an egg with a little milk, pepper, salt, and spice. Cut some slices of bread all of the same size and shape, dip them in the mixture and fry them a light brown in butter or oil. Drain on paper, pile high on a dish, and serve with tomato sauce. Another way is to dip them in milk only, and then cover them with egg and a mixture of bread crumbs, lemon-peel, sweet herbs, and chopped parsley, before frying them as above.

FRENCH TOAST.

One egg, beaten into a cup of milk, with a tablespoonful of sugar. Dip in slices of bread and fry a light brown, in hot lard. Eat with butter, or sugar and milk.

RAISED BISCUIT.

Half a cup of shortening, one pint of milk, a half teaspoonful of salt, half a Vienna yeast-cake, two teaspoonfuls of sugar and flour. Boil the milk, and pour it over the ingredients, with the exception of yeast-cake and flour. When the mixture cools down to a tepid condition, add enough flour to make a batter; pour the yeast-cake, which must have been soaked in a little water, into the batter; cover, and set aside to rise. When light, mix up pretty stiff with flour, and set aside to rise again. When light a second time, mould on the board, cut out cakes, place them in the pan, and let them rise. Then bake in an ordinary oven.

SODA BISCUIT.—NO. I.

One pint of flour, a piece of butter the size of an egg, one cup of milk, salt, two teaspoonfuls of cream tartar, and one of soda.

SODA BISCUIT.—NO. II.

Three pints of flour, two teaspoonfuls of cream tartar, and a small teaspoonful of salt, put through a sieve. One teaspoonful of lard, one of butter, rubbed through the flour, a small tablespoonful of powdered sugar, one pint of milk, one teaspoonful of soda, dissolved in a little milk, and then mixed with the rest of the pint; stir up lightly, and roll very lightly. Bake in a quick oven about fifteen minutes.

PLAIN SODA BISCUIT.

One quart of flour, a teaspoonful of soda and two of cream tartar, half a teaspoonful of salt, a lump of butter the size of an egg. Mix to form a soft dough, roll out, and bake quickly.

WISCONSIN BISCUIT.

One pint each of milk and graham flour, two eggs, one desertspoonful of sugar. Bake in a muffin-pan or rings, after beating thoroughly.

POTATO ROLLS.

Four large potatoes, one tablespoonful of butter, half a teaspoonful of salt, half a pint of milk, half a teacupful of yeast, or half of a Vienna yeast-cake and flour. Boil the potatoes, peel and mash them, add the butter and salt while they are hot, then the milk. Add the yeast and flour while the mixture is lukewarm. Knead and set away to rise; as soon as it is light, roll out the biscuit; place them in a well-buttered pan, and let them rise. Bake in a pretty warm oven.

GRAHAM ROLLS.

One quart of graham flour, one quart of wheat flour, a pint and a half of tepid water, one gill of molasses, one gill of yeast, two ounces of butter, two teaspoonfuls of salt. Mix thoroughly together with a spoon and leave in a warm place to rise; when light, drop into buttered roll-pans and bake. Mix at night for breakfast.

GRAHAM GEMS.—NO. I.

One pint of sour milk, one egg, one spoonful of sugar, a pinch of salt, a teaspoonful of soda, and enough good, fresh graham flour to make a stiff batter. Bake in greased gem-pans, or pour the batter into a large bread-pan and bake like gingerbread. They will be delicious, light, puffy, and wholesome.

GRAHAM GEMS.—NO. II.

One quart of graham flour, half a teacupful of molasses, one teacup of yeast, a little salt. Stir up soft, over night with tepid water. In the morning bake in gem-pans.

GRAHAM GEMS.—NO. III.

One pint graham flour, one small cupful of brown sugar, one teaspoonful of salt, three small teaspoonfuls of baking powder, lard the size of an egg. Rub well together with the hands; then add one egg, well beaten, and half a pint of milk. Beat thoroughly and bake in hot pans.

OATMEAL GEMS.

One cup of oatmeal; soak over night in one cup of water; in the morning, add one cup of sour milk, one teaspoonful of saleratus (or sweet milk and baking powder), three tablespoonfuls of brown sugar, a little salt. Flour enough to make a stiff batter. Bake in gem-irons. If on first trial they are moist and sticky, add more flour next time. They can also be made from oatmeal porridge.

WAFFLES, SHORTCAKE, ETC.

BLACKBERRY SHORTCAKE.

Prepare a dough as for soda biscuit, only use double the quantity of shortening. Roll an inch and a half thick, and after baking, split; butter on both sides, and, having mashed the berries raw with sugar, lay on all that the cake will hold. If a raised crust is preferred, knead enough butter or lard into common bread-dough to make it very short, divide into two parts, and roll each one less than an inch thick; butter the top of one piece, lay the other on it, and set in a favorable place to rise. When very light, bake. The two crusts will easily separate from each other, and if the under one is lightly picked up with a fork it will better absorb the juice. Pile the blackberries crushed with sugar between, and eat with sweetened cream.

STRAWBERRY SHORTCAKE.—NO. I.

One quart of flour, two-thirds of a cup of shortening, salt, two teaspoonfuls of best baking powder. Mix with water or milk. Make the cake about one and a-half or two inches thick, so that it may be split readily when baked. Butter the parts while warm. Sugar the berries an hour previous, and when the cake is ready, split it and place the fruit between the halves and on top. Cream can be poured over all, if desired.

STRAWBERRY SHORTCAKE.—NO. II.

Mix one quart of flour with one teaspoonful of salt, four well-beaten eggs, and a teacupful of thick cream, or melted butter. Make two layers, each a quarter of an inch, and bake together. When done split them and place between the halves a layer of sugared strawberries, and another layer on top of the same. Have ready about a pint of berries, mashed thoroughly with half a cupful of water and plenty of sugar, as a sauce to pour over it when served.

WAFFLES.—NO. I.

One pint of milk, three eggs, a piece of butter the size of a walnut. Rub into flour enough to make a soft batter. Half a teaspoonful of soda, and three-quarters of a teaspoonful of cream tartar.

WAFFLES.—NO. II.

Half a cupful of butter, four cups of flour, four eggs, one teaspoonful soda, two teaspoonfuls of cream tartar. Milk sufficient for a thin batter. Rub the soda and cream of tartar in the flour; then rub in the butter. Beat the yolks and whites of the eggs separately, adding the whites last. Eat with powdered sugar and cinnamon.

BREAKFAST WAFFLES.

After breakfast stir into the hominy that is left one teaspoonful of butter and a little salt. Set it aside. The next morning thin it with milk, and add two eggs, beaten well. Stir in flour enough to make of the right consistency, and bake in waffle irons.

POP-OVERS.

One egg, one cup of flour, one cup of milk, one tablespoonful each of salt and melted butter. Beat the yolk and white separately, and very light. Mix the yolk, salt, butter and milk together ; then the flour gently, and lastly, the white of the egg. Have the gem-pan very hot in the oven, drop into each a small piece of butter.

BREAKFAST PUFFS.

One pint of milk, two eggs, well beaten, a pint and a half of flour, a small piece of butter. If the milk is sour, add half a teaspoonful of soda. Bake in muffin-pans.

QUICK MUFFINS.

One pint of sour cream, one pint of flour, three eggs, a pinch of salt, a teaspoonful of soda dissolved in warm water. Add the soda to the cream, then the yolks of the eggs, add the flour and beat very light. Lastly the whites of the eggs, beaten stiff.

MUFFINS.—NO. I.

One pint of milk, one egg, two tablespoonfuls of sugar, a piece of butter half as large as an egg, two teaspoonfuls of cream tartar, one teaspoonful of soda. Flour to make a stiff batter. Bake in rings in a very quick oven.

MUFFINS.—NO. II.

One cup of milk, three eggs, one tablespoonful of butter, two tablespoonfuls of sugar, one teaspoonful of soda, two teaspoonfuls of cream tartar, salt. Mix the soda and cream tartar in flour separately. Make stiff as for cake.

CORN MEAL MUFFINS.

Half a pound of white corn meal, one-half pound of flour, one tablespoonful of sugar, one tablespoonful of butter, three teaspoonfuls of baking powder, two eggs beaten separately. Mix with enough sweet milk to make a batter, and bake in muffin-rings forty-five minutes.

RAISED MUFFINS.

Melt about two ounces of butter in a quart of warm milk. If the milk is then too warm for the eggs and

WAFFLES, SHORTCAKE, ETC.—FRITTERS.   57

yeast, cool it by stirring in several handfuls of flour, then add three eggs, well beaten, three tablespoonfuls of yeast, and a little salt ; add enough flour to make it so stiff that a spoon will nearly stand in it. Beat well, and let it rise about three hours.

SALLY LUNN.

One quart of flour, two eggs, two cups of milk, three tablespoonfuls of sugar, a piece of butter the size of an egg, two teaspoonfuls of cream tartar, one teaspoonful of soda, a little salt. Stir the cream tartar, salt and sugar into the flour ; add the eggs without beating, the butter melted and one cup of milk. Dissolve the soda in another cup of milk and stir all together. Bake in pans the size of breakfast plates.

SPANISH BUN.

One-quarter of a pound of butter, one-quarter of a pound of currants, two and a half cups of flour, one cup of sugar, two eggs.

RUSK.

Make a sponge of two teacups of milk, one cup of yeast, salt and flour enough for a stiff batter. Let it rise at noon. In the evening, mix in one cup of butter, two cups of sugar and two eggs, well beaten. Let it stand all night to rise. In the morning, mould it into cakes with the hands, put them into pans so as not to touch each other at first. Let them rise again, then bake. A little cinnamon may be added if desired.

FRITTERS, GRIDDLE CAKES, ETC.

GREEN CORN FRITTERS.—NO. I.

Twelve ears of sweet corn, grated, one teaspoonful of salt, one teaspoonful of pepper, one egg beaten into two tablespoonfuls of flour. Mix thoroughly and drop into hot lard.

CORN FRITTERS.—NO. II.

One dozen ears of corn, grated, four eggs, one teaspoonful of baking powder, one cup of milk, one tablespoonful of melted butter, a cup and a half of flour. Mix well together and fry in boiling butter and lard, equal parts of each.

FRITTERS.

Two-thirds of a cup of sour milk, half a teaspoonful of soda, one tablespoonful of sugar, a little salt. Flour to make a thick batter.

CORN OYSTERS.

Three dozen ears of large, young corn, six eggs, one saltspoon of salt. Grate the corn, which must be tender, from the cob as fine as possible, and dredge with flour. Beat the eggs very light and mix gradually with the corn, then give the whole a good hard beating. Have ready lard and butter in a frying-pan. When this is boiling hot put in portions of the mixture in oval cakes to resemble oysters ; fry brown and serve hot.

APPLE FRITTERS.

Three eggs ; one tablespoonful of sugar ; one pint of milk ; juice and grated rind of half a lemon ; one-half pound of chopped apples ; one-half pound of sifted flour ; one teaspoonful of salt. Beat the eggs very light, add the sugar and lemon, then the milk, flour and salt, and finally the apples. Stir well together, and drop by the large spoonful into boiling lard.

OYSTER FRITTERS.

To the liquor of the oysters add the same quantity of milk, three eggs, a little salt, and flour enough for a batter. Chop the oysters and stir in the batter. Cook in butter and lard. The fat must be very hot, and the fritters cooked to a fine yellow brown. Some prefer to bake them upon a griddle, the same as cakes.

CLAM FRITTERS.

Four eggs, one cup of milk, one cup of broth; stir in flour to make a thin batter. Chop the clams fine, add to the batter and fry in spoonfuls. Oysters are nice served in the same way.

BLACKBERRY FRITTERS.

Make a batter of sour milk or cream, as for pancakes, only quite stiff. If cream is used, allow one more egg than for sour milk, then stir thick with blackberries. Have ready a kettle of hot lard; dip a tablespoon into the lard, then drop a spoonful of batter into the lard; the grease will prevent the batter from sticking to the spoon, and will let it drop off in nice oval shapes. Eat with syrup.

MOCK OYSTERS.

One pint of grated corn, one egg, one small teacupful of flour, half a cupful of butter or cream, salt and pepper. Mix all well together and fry to a light brown. When done, butter. A tablespoonful of batter will be about the size of an oyster.

BREAD GRIDDLE CAKES.

Soak over night as much bread as a pint of milk will moisten. Rub it smooth in the morning. Add a teacupful of flour, two eggs, a little sugar, one tablespoonful of Indian meal; one teaspoonful of soda in a small half teacup of water, and use two teaspoonfuls of the water.

WHEAT GRIDDLE CAKES.

One quart of flour; one tablespoonful of sugar; one teaspoonful of salt; two large spoonfuls of Royal baking powder; two eggs; a pint and a half of milk. Sift together the flour, sugar, salt, and baking powder; add the beaten eggs and milk; mix to form a smooth batter. Bake on a good hot griddle. Serve with maple syrup.

INDIAN MEAL CAKES.

One pint of Indian meal ; one gill of boiling milk ; one teaspoonful of butter ; salt to taste ; one gill of wheat flour ; one gill of yeast ; two eggs ; milk sufficient to make a batter. Cut up the butter in the Indian meal and add the salt ; then stir into it the boiling milk. Beat the eggs and when the meal is cool, add them and the wheat flour, with as much milk as will form a batter. Add the yeast last. When the batter is light bake on the griddle.

SCOTCH CRUMPETS.

Three eggs ; one pint and a half of milk ; a small piece of butter ; as much oatmeal or graham flour as will make a batter ; salt, and half a cupful of yeast, or half a yeast cake. Have the milk warm, in which melt the butter. It must be very nearly cold when the eggs, well beaten, are added, then stir in the flour and salt, add the yeast, beat well and stand it away to rise. Bake on a griddle.

BUCKWHEAT CAKES.

One quart of buckwheat flour and a scant teaspoonful of salt. Add warm water sufficient for a batter. Beat thoroughly ; then add two tablespoonfuls of baker's yeast, and let rise over night.

BUCKWHEAT CAKES.—NO. II.

One quart of buckwheat flour, into which stir lukewarm milk sufficient for a thin batter ; add half a tablespoonful of salt and beat thoroughly. Then add a small cupful of Indian meal, and two tablespoonfuls of yeast. Set it where it will keep warm through the night, and in the morning add a teaspoonful of soda, dissolved in a little warm water.

RICE CAKES.

One scant pint of cold boiled rice, soaked over night in a pint of milk or water. One pint of milk added in the morning; one pint of flour stirred into the rice and milk; two eggs, well beaten. Half a teaspoonful of soda dissolved in a little warm water; one teaspoonful of salt. More milk can be added if needed.

PIES.

PIE CRUST.

Three coffeecupfuls of flour; one teacupful of lard; salt; cut with a knife, and stir together with a little ice-water. Makes three pies.

PIE CRUST.—NO. II.

One pound of flour and half a pound of butter, or butter and lard, mixed with a little salt, make a very good crust.

APPLE CUSTARD PIES.

Three cupfuls of stewed apples, nearly a cupful of white sugar; six eggs; one quart of milk. Make the stewed apple very sweet and let it cool. Beat the eggs light, and mix the yolks well with the apple, seasoning with nutmeg only. Then stir in gradually the milk, beating constantly. Add the whites of the eggs last. Fill your crust and bake without a top crust.

TO PRESERVE PUMPKIN.

Take good, ripe pumpkins, pare, and stew as dry as possible; place in the oven on a sheet of tin, and let it remain until thoroughly dried, not baked; then store away in a dry place, and it will keep an indefinite time. It only requires to be soaked in milk a few hours before using.

PUMPKIN PIES.

One quart of pumpkin, well cooked and sifted; two quarts and a pint of milk; one teaspoonful of salt; four teaspoonfuls of ginger; two teaspoonfuls of nutmeg; two teaspoonfuls of cloves; ten eggs; sugar to taste.

MINCE PIES, PLAIN.

One cupful each of chopped raisins, sugar, molasses, and vinegar; one tablespoonful of cinnamon; one teaspoonful of cloves; a cupful and a half of soda crackers, broken; two cupfuls of boiling water; a little salt. This will make three pies.

MINCE PIES, VERY RICH.

Two pounds of beef, boiled tender and chopped very fine; two pounds of apples, chopped; one pound and a half each of currants and raisins; one pound of citron. Add plenty of sugar, all kinds of spices, and two quarts of cider. Set it away for a week or ten days, and if too dry, add more cider.

CHERRY PIES.

After moulding out the crust and fitting it to the pie plates, having washed the cherries (cooking cherries are the best), spread them on the paste with a bountiful supply of sugar over them and bake with a top crust.

PEACH PIE.

Cover the pie-plates with a nice, rich crust. Then add a layer of peaches and a layer of sugar, until pretty well piled up. No top crust is required. Canned or fresh peaches make a delicious pie, and for variety they can be made into a peach shortcake, after the recipe for strawberry shortcake.

LEMON PIE.—NO. I.

Two tablespoonfuls of corn starch, wet with cold water; pour on two cups of boiling water; two tablespoonfuls of butter, two cups of sugar, juice and rind of two lemons, two eggs. Set on the stove to thicken.

CAKE FOR SAME.—Three cups of flour, two cups of

sugar, one large spoonful of butter, two eggs, one cup of milk, two teaspoonfuls of cream tartar, one teaspoonful of soda. Bake in jelly-cake plates. Cut the center out and fill with the above custard.

LEMON PIE.—NO. II.

Two cups of sugar, two lemons, six eggs, one cup of milk, one tablespoonful of flour. Beat the whites of the eggs with four tablespoonfuls of sugar; spread this on the pies after they are baked; return to the oven and brown.

LEMON PIE.—NO. III.

Two lemons, two teacups of sugar, half a cup of molasses, one cup of water, two tablespoonfuls of flour, one tablespoonful of butter. Slice the lemons as thin as possible; mix all the ingredients together. Set over the fire, and let them come to a boil. Cool before filling the crust.

LEMON PIE.—NO IV.

The juice and the yellow part of the rind of two lemons, two cups of sugar, the yolks of four eggs, four tablespoonfuls of flour, two cupfuls of water; cook the mixture until well thickened. Bake the pastry, then pour in the mixture, beat the whites of four eggs to a froth, add two teaspoonfuls of sugar, then spread over the top of the pies, and place in the oven until brown. Enough for two pies.

LEMON CREAM PIE.

One teacupful of powdered sugar, one tablespoonful of butter, one egg, one lemon—juice and grated rind, removing the seeds with care; one teacupful of boiling water, one tablespoonful of corn starch mixed with cold water; stir the corn starch into the water, cream the butter and sugar and pour over them the hot mixture; when quite cool, add lemon and beaten egg; take the inner rind off the lemon and mince very small ; bake in an open shell.

MARIA'S THREE CREAM PIES.

Three eggs and one teaspoonful of cream tartar, one cup of white sugar, half a teaspoonful of soda, a cupful and a half of flour ; a little salt. Dissolve the soda in a tablespoonful of sweet milk ; beat the eggs and sugar together for five minutes, then add milk and soda ; then the flour and cream tartar.

Cream for the Pies.

One pint of milk, two eggs, one cupful of white sugar, two tablespoonfuls of corn starch ; flavoring. Mix the corn starch with a little of the milk, then add eggs and remainder of the milk and flavoring. Let it boil up three or four times, stirring all the time. To be put into the pies when cold.

COCOANUT PIES.

One cocoanut, grated, half a pound of butter, four eggs, three-quarters of a pound of sugar, two slices of stale baker's bread soaked in boiled milk ; add half a pint of boiled milk.

SWEET POTATO PIE.

Two common-sized sweet potatoes, one tablespoonful of butter, half a cupful each of sugar and sweet milk, three eggs. Boil the potatoes and mash fine with the butter. Then mix in the sugar and milk. Break in the eggs and stir thoroughly. Make a good pie-crust and pour in the mixture. Enough for two pies.

APPLE CUSTARD PIES.

One pint of milk, three eggs, one pint of apple-sauce, one cupful of sugar ; lemon. Beat the apple-sauce until entirely smooth and free from lumps ; then stir in the milk, add the sugar and the eggs, well beaten. Flavor with lemon ; bake with under crust only.

PUDDINGS.

QUEEN OF PUDDINGS.

One pint of bread crumbs, one lemon, one quart of milk; a piece of butter the size of an egg, two cups of sugar, four eggs ; jelly. Mix the bread crumbs, the milk, the yolks of the eggs, the grated rind of the lemon, one cupful of sugar and the butter thoroughly, and bake for half an hour. Beat the whites of the eggs stiff with a teacupful of sugar, and the juice of the lemon. Spread a layer of jelly or preserves over the pudding, then the whites of the eggs, and return to the oven until slightly brown.

GRAHAM PUDDING.

Two cupfuls of graham flour, one cupful each of molasses, milk and raisins, two eggs, one teaspoonful each of soda, cloves and cinnamon; a little nutmeg. Steam three hours.

APPLE TARTS.

Stew eight tart apples as if for sauce; sweeten, and add cinnamon and a tablespoonful of butter while hot ; when cold, add half a teacupful of bread crumbs and the yolks of four eggs, well beaten, with a cupful of sweet milk. Bake with under crust; when done, beat the whites of the eggs and four large spoonfuls of white sugar, and flavoring extract to suit the taste. Beat stiff, pour over the tarts, set them in the oven until of a light brown.

HURRY-SCURRY PUDDING.

Cut a stale French roll in slices rather more than half an inch thick, and soak in milk flavored with vanilla, or any essence that may be liked. Place the slices on a strainer, and then fry a bright golden-brown color. Arrange neatly in a dish, and pour over all some jam sauce ; or the slices can be served with powdered sugar instead of sauce. Any pieces of light bread can be used.

MINUTE PUDDING.

One pint of milk, five tablespoonfuls of flour, five eggs. Beat the yolks of the eggs, and add to the flour and milk ; then stir in the well-beaten whites very lightly. Bake in a quick oven. Eat with dip of milk, sweetened, thickened and flavored to taste.

GREEN CORN PUDDING.

One dozen ears of green corn, grated ; one egg, well beaten ; one pint of rich milk, one tablespoonful of sugar, a lump of butter the size of a walnut, salt and pepper. Pour into a dish, and bake half an hour. Send hot to the table. To be eaten as a vegetable.

PLUM PUDDING, CHEAP.

One cup of suet, one cup of raisins, one cup of currants, one cup of sweet milk, half a cup of molasses, three and a half cups of flour, one egg, one teaspoonful of soda, a little salt. Boil three hours.

PLUM PUDDING, ENGLISH.

One pound each of currants and stoned raisins, dredged with flour, a quarter of a pound of beef suet, chopped fine, one pound of bread crumbs, a quarter of a pound of citron, eight eggs, half a pint of milk, one gill of sweet cider, one large coffeecup of sugar, one teaspoonful of of salt, mace and nutmeg to suit the taste. Beat the whites of the eggs to a stiff froth and add last. Boil seven hours in a bag, turn it several times while cooking. To be eaten with a rich sauce.

PLUM PUDDING, CHRISTMAS.

One quart of milk, six eggs, three-quarters of a pound of suet, one pound and a quarter each of raisins (stoned) and currants, a quarter of a pound of citron, one nutmeg, allspice, cloves, cinnamon and salt to taste, two tablespoonfuls of molasses, a wineglass of sweet cider, flour sufficient to make a thick batter. Boil in a cloth from eight to ten hours, leaving room to swell.

BATTER PUDDING.

Four eggs, three half pints of milk, half a cupful each of seedless raisins and currants, two teaspoonfuls of Rumford yeast powder, mixed in the flour, one pound and a quarter of flour. Beat the eggs light, add the flour and milk gradually, stir in the fruit ; a little salt ; boil two hours. When fruit is in season, instead of raisins and currants, add one quart of raspberries or other fruit. Eat with sauce.

ENGLISH EGGLESS PUDDING.

One pound of carrots, boiled and grated, one pound of suet, chopped fine, one pound each of raisins and currants, one pound of flour, two ounces of citron, two tea-cupfuls of molasses, one grated nutmeg. To be steamed or boiled three hours.

SUET PUDDING QUICKLY MADE.

Three eggs, six ounces of suet, one pound of flour, one-third of a pound each of raisins and currants, one ounce of candied lemon-peel or citron, two ounces of sugar, half a teaspoonful of ground allspice. Make a stiff batter with water. Place in a steamer, or boil one hour and a half.

FIG PUDDING.

Half a pound of figs, one full cup of bread crumbs, one cup of brown sugar, one cup of suet, half a cup of milk, half teaspoonful of soda, two tablespoonfuls of sweet cider, two eggs, a little nutmeg. To be steamed in a mould.

CHARLOTTE PUDDING.

Remove the crust from a loaf of bread, dip the slices in milk and spread with butter. Pare and cut apples very thin. Lay the bread in a buttered dish, spread over it the apples, sweeten and flavor with the juice and grated rind of a lemon. Bake until the apples are tender.

HUCKLEBERRY PUDDING.

Cover the bottom of a pudding dish with slices of buttered bread. Cover the bread with a generous supply of huckleberries, and sugar them, then add more slices of bread, more berries and sugar, having the last layer bread. Finally add a cupful of water; cover the dish with a plate, and bake for one hour. Eat with sauce.

PEACH PUDDING.

Cut up the peaches, remove skins and stones, lay in a pudding dish, sprinkle over them half a cup of sugar; make a boiled custard of one pint of milk, the yolks of two eggs, half a cup of sugar, two tablespoonfuls of corn starch; scald the milk before pouring in this mixture; salt. Pour this over the peaches; beat the whites of the two eggs, with a tablespoonful of pulverized sugar; pour this over the pudding, and brown in a hot oven. Canned peaches may be used if desired, and oranges can be treated same way.

APPLE DUMPLINGS.—NO. I.

Rub together a quarter of a pound of butter, a pound of flour and a little salt. Core, pare and slice one dozen apples. Have ready a dozen small cloths well floured, on each of which lay paste enough for one dumpling, and sufficient apples. Take the four corners and tie a string around them close to the dumpling. To insure their being light, just before putting them into the boiling water, throw in a cupful of cold water, which will stop the boiling long enough to give them a chance to rise.

APPLE DUMPLINGS.—NO. II.

Take tart, mellow apples, pare, remove the core, and fill the place with sugar; then take one quart of flour, two or three teaspoonfuls of baking powder, and half a tablespoonful of shortening; mix with sweet milk or water—mix as soft as possible—and roll it out; cut in squares of sufficient size to hold the apples; set on a plate and place in the steamer.

A DELICATE PUDDING.

Three tablespoonfuls of corn starch mixed in a little cold water. Have one pint of water boiling on the stove; into this stir the corn starch and the well-beaten whites of three eggs; let it boil up once; pour it into an earthen pudding dish which will hold three pints; steam the pudding for ten minutes. For the sauce use the yolks of the three eggs, one cupful of sweet milk, and a small piece of butter; boil for a few minutes; when cool, flavor with lemon or vanilla. The pudding is to be eaten cold also.

PRUNE PUDDING.

Heat a little more than a pint of sweet milk to the boiling point, then stir in gradually a little cold milk in which you have rubbed smooth a heaping tablespoonful of corn starch; add sugar to suit the taste; three well-beaten eggs, about a teaspoonful of butter, and a little grated nutmeg. Let this come to a boil, then pour it into a buttered pudding dish, first adding a cupful of stewed prunes, with the stones taken out. Bake for fifteen or twenty minutes, according to the state of the oven. Serve with or without sauce. A little cream improves it if poured over it when placed in saucers.

COTTAGE PUDDING.

One cupful of sugar, one tablespoonful of butter; two eggs; one cupful of sweet milk; three cupfuls of flour, or enough to make a tolerably stiff batter; half a teaspoonful of soda; one teaspoonful of cream tartar, sifted with the flour; one teaspoonful of salt; rub the butter and sugar together, beat in the yolks of the eggs, then the milk and soda, the salt and beaten whites, alternately with flour; bake in buttered mould and eat with liquid sauce.

RHUBARB PUDDING.

To one quart of buttermilk add one egg, one large teaspoonful of soda, and flour enough to make a thick batter. Have ready half a dozen stalks of rhubarb, cut up fine; stir it in the batter. Tie it tightly in a bag, drop it into a kettle of boiling water, and let it boil an hour. Serve with cream and sugar.

MERINGUE PUDDING.

One pint of milk, four tablespoonfuls of powdered crackers; three eggs; a small piece of butter; a little salt. Separate the whites and the yolks of the eggs; beat the whites to a stiff froth; add a teacupful of sugar; flavor with vanilla, and spread over the pudding when cool; set in the oven to brown slightly.

SPONGE PUDDING.

Half a cup of sugar; half a cup of butter; one cup of flour, one cup of milk (exactly); six eggs beaten separately. Mix the flour smooth with a little of the milk. Boil the rest of the milk and stir the mixed flour into it, and pour it over the butter and sugar (well beaten), and set to cool an hour. Before rising, add the yolks of the six eggs, and the whites beaten stiff. Put the dish in a pan of hot water, and bake an hour. Eat hot with sauce.

RICE PUDDING.

Two quarts of milk; a small teacupful of rice; three tablespoonfuls of sugar, a piece of butter the size of an egg; a little salt; a little grated nutmeg on the top. Bake in a slow oven, stirring it every twenty minutes, for two hours, after which let it come to a pretty brown.

This is good either warm or cold. Give it time to lose some of its heat before serving.

ORANGE PUDDING.

Five oranges ; one pint of milk ; one large cupful of sugar ; three eggs ; one tablespoonful of corn starch. Peel the oranges, which must be sweet and juicy, and cut them into thin slices, taking out all the seeds. Pour the white sugar over them. Let the milk get boiling hot by setting it in boiling water, then add the yolks of the eggs, well beaten, and the corn starch, made smooth with a little cold milk. Stir all the time, and as soon as it thickens pour it over the fruit. Beat the whites of the eggs to a stiff froth with a teaspoonful of sugar, and spread over the top of the pudding, setting it in the oven for about five minutes.

LEMON PUDDING.

Two lemons ; one quart of milk ; a cupful and a half of sugar ; two tablespoonfuls of pounded crackers ; three eggs ; half a cupful of melted butter. Mix the grated rind and juice of the lemons with the sugar. Beat the eggs thoroughly and stir into the juice and sugar. Mix the cracker with the milk, then beat all together, and turn into a dish lined with puff-paste. Bake twenty or thirty minutes. To be eaten cold.

ECONOMICAL PUDDING.

Two tablespoonfuls of rice ; one saltspoonful of salt ; two ounces of butter ; four tablespoonfuls of tapioca ; one and a half pint of milk ; two eggs ; sugar and nutmeg to taste. Boil the rice in a small saucepan with as much water as it will absorb. When boiled enough, add the salt. Then set it by the fire until the rice is quite soft and dry. Toss it up in a dish ; add two ounces of butter ; four tablespoonfuls of tapioca, previously soaked, and the other ingredients. Stir all together and bake one hour.

SNOWDON PUDDING.

One-half pound each of beef suet, bread crumbs, raisins and sugar, two tablespoonfuls of orange marmalade ; three eggs. Shred the suet very fine. Beat the eggs thoroughly, mix all together and boil three hours. Eat with sauce.

TAPIOCA PUDDING.

Eight tablespoonfuls of tapioca, five eggs, one quart of milk ; spice and sugar to taste ; two tablespoonfuls of melted butter, juice of one lemon. Soak the tapioca until soft, in the warmed milk, then add the butter, the eggs, well beaten, and other ingredients. Bake in a buttered dish.

RICE CUP PUDDINGS.

One teacupful of rice, two ounces of butter, one quart of milk, three eggs, one pint of cream ; sugar and nutmeg to taste. Pick and wash the rice, boil it in the milk until very thick and dry ; add the cream and the butter while hot. When it is sufficiently cool add the eggs, well beaten, and sugar, about three tablespoonfuls. Butter the cups, pour in the mixture, and bake in a moderate oven. Grate nutmeg over the top and serve with cream.

PEACH BAKED PUDDING.

Line a deep pudding dish with thin slices of baker's bread. Fill up the dish with ripe peaches or canned fruit, cut in pieces and sugared. Cover the top with thin slices of bread, buttered and dipped in the yolk of an egg, well beaten. Bake and serve with milk or cream.

FARMER'S APPLE PUDDING.

Stew some apples tender--if juicy, with very little water ; add to one pound of the apple, whilst hot, a quarter of a pound of butter, and sugar to the taste. Beat four eggs, and stir in when the apple is cold. Butter the bottom and sides of a deep pudding dish, cover with bread crumbs, add the mixture, and strew bread crumbs thickly over the top. Set it in a tolerably hot oven, and when baked sift sugar over the top.

BREAD AND BUTTER PUDDING.

Spread butter on some thin slices of bread. As they are ready, lay them in a dish, and between the slices strew some currants, with a very little chopped lemon or orange peel; have a quart of milk ready, with four eggs beaten in it; pour it gently over the bread; let it stand for an hour, and then bake.

SMALL FRUIT PUDDINGS.

Make a batter as if for waffles; to one pint of milk allow two eggs, and enough flour to thicken; one teaspoonful of baking powder should be stirred into the flour. Fill a sufficient number of custard cups with this and fruit in layers. Then set the cups in the steamer, and let the water boil underneath it for a full hour. If there is no steamer at hand, set the cups in a large pan of hot water in the oven. Serve while hot, with sugar and cream. Any jam is nice for this, as are raw apples chopped fine.

CREAM PUFFS.

Half a cupful of butter, one cupful of hot water, one cupful of flour, three eggs. Melt the butter in the hot water, and while boiling beat in the flour, then take off the stove and cool. When cool stir in three eggs, one at a time, without beating; drop on tins quickly, and bake about twenty-five minutes in a moderate oven. When the puffs are baked, open the side of each, and fill with the following custard : Half a pint of milk, three tablespoonfuls of sugar, one egg, two large tablespoonfuls of flour, lemon or other flavoring. Make same as boiled custard.

PARADISE PUDDING.

Three apples, three ounces of currants, one-quarter pound of bread crumbs, half the rind of a lemon, three eggs, two tablespoonfuls of cider, three ounces of sugar, salt, nutmeg. Pare, core, and mince the apples into small pieces. Mix them with the bread crumbs, the eggs well beaten, the sugar, currants, lemon rind, and cider, with salt and grated nutmeg to taste. Pour the pudding into a buttered mould, tie down with a cloth and boil for two hours, or cover the pudding dish with an inverted plate and steam in an oven an hour, perhaps a little more. Serve hot with sweet sauce.

GREEN CORN PUDDING.

Twelve ears of corn, one tablespoonful sugar, one quart of milk, one tablespoonful flour, two eggs, two teaspoonfuls of salt. Grate the corn. Beat the eggs thoroughly. Mix the flour well with a little of the milk; then mix it all together and bake four hours. Eat with sugar and butter, or with pudding sauce.

ANNIE'S APPLE TAPIOCA.

One coffee cup of tapioca, rind of one lemon, nine apples, one-half teaspoonful of salt, one-half cup of sugar. Soak the tapioca one hour in a quart of cold water ; add the salt ; core the apples and with them cover a pudding dish. Skim the tapioca, and add the sugar. Grate the rind of the lemon over the apples, and then pour the tapioca over them. Bake until the apples are soft, and then cover with a meringue. Eat with pudding sauce or with sugar and cream.

SAGO PUDDING.

Four tablespoonfuls of sago, one pint and a half of milk, four eggs, three tablespoonfuls of sugar, grated lemon peel, cinnamon, nutmeg. Boil the sago in the milk, and when cool add the eggs, thoroughly beaten with the sugar, add the other ingredients, and bake slowly.

JENNY LIND'S PUDDING.

Grate half a loaf of bread.   Butter the pudding dish and place in it a layer of crumbs, then a layer of apples cut into small pieces, and covered with sugar; then a layer of bread crumbs, alternately, until the dish is full. Scatter a few bits of butter on top, and bake.

SAUCES FOR PUDDINGS.

BROWN PUDDING SAUCE.

One cupful of sugar, half a cupful of butter, the yolk of one egg and the whites of two eggs. Stir the sugar, butter and yolk to a cream; add the whites and a little nutmeg.

SAUCE FOR BOILED RICE.

One cup of sugar, the yolks of three eggs, one teacupful of sweet cream, the juice and grated rind of two lemons.

HARD SAUCE.

Two tablespoonfuls of butter, ten tablespoonfuls of sugar. Rub thoroughly together; mould in form in a small dish and grate nutmeg over the top.

HOT SAUCE.

Six tablespoonfuls of sugar, two of butter, and one egg; beat the butter, sugar and the yolk of the egg together, then add the white beaten to a froth; lastly stir in a teacupful of boiling water and a teaspoonful of the extract of vanilla.

PLAIN PUDDING SAUCE.

Half a cupful of butter, one cupful of white sugar; beat together very light; flavor to taste. Fifteen minutes before serving, set the bowl on a pan of hot water on the range, and stir until hot. It will raise in a white foam to the top of the bowl.

WHIPPED CREAM SAUCE.

Whip the cream ten minutes, then sweeten to the taste and add a little salt.

LEMON SAUCE.

One cupful of sugar, half a cupful of butter, half of a large tablespoonful of flour, one pint of boiling water, one sliced lemon.

LIGHT DESSERTS.

ORANGE CUSTARD.

Cut half a dozen oranges into small pieces, and remove the seeds. Then pour over them a boiled custard made as follows : Set over the fire one quart of milk, sweetened, and let it come to a boil. Then remove from the fire and add a spoonful at a time of the yolks of three eggs, well beaten. Return to the fire until thickened to the consistency of cream. Flavor with vanilla and pour over the oranges in a glass dish. Beat the whites of the eggs stiff with powdered sugar, flavor slightly and drop with a spoon into a pan of boiling water. These spoonfuls will soon cook and become firm. Remove them, cool a moment, and then pile them on the custard and oranges.

ORANGE CREAM.

Make a custard with the yolks of eight eggs, four ounces of powdered sugar and the thin rind of two oranges. Stir it in a saucepan until it thickens. Dissolve one ounce of gelatine in a little warm water and add to it the juice of one orange. Add this to the custard, strain it into a mould and place it on the ice to set.

BLACKBERRY FLUMMERY.

Stew three pints of berries with one of sugar. To a teacupful of ground rice, arrowroot, or corn starch, add enough water to soften it. When the berries have stewed about fifteen minutes, stir in the rice, and continue stirring until thick. Eat cold with sweetened cream.

PINEAPPLE SHERBET.

To one can of pineapple allow a pint of sugar and one heaping tablespoonful of gelatine ; chop the pineapple very fine, add the juice from the can, and the sugar. Soak the gelatine for an hour or more, until soft, in cold water ; then add half a cupful of boiling water ; stir this in with the pineapple. Let it stand until cold.

LEMON SPONGE.

Soak one ounce of gelatine in one pint of cold water for five minutes, then dissolve it by heating over the fire. Add the rind of two lemons, three-quarters of a pound of lump sugar, and the juice of three lemons ; boil all together two minutes, steam it, and let it remain until nearly cold, then add the whites of two eggs, well beaten, and whisk it well ten minutes ; put it lightly into a glass dish.

CUSTARDS—BAKED.

One quart of milk, three tablespoonfuls of sugar, four eggs ; nutmeg. Beat the eggs to a froth, add the sugar, and then mix thoroughly with the milk ; flavor with vanilla. Pour the custard into cups, grate nutmeg over each, and then place them in a dripping-pan in which is half an inch of water, and bake in a good oven.

APPLE OMELET.

Six large apples, two ounces of butter, four ounces of sugar, three eggs, two tablespoonfuls of cream. Boil, mash and strain the apples, stir in the butter and sugar, working until entirely smooth and cold ; add the eggs, beaten as light as possible, with the cream, and whip all well together. Warm a baking dish, butter the sides and bottom, and sprinkle with bread crumbs ; pour in the omelet, bake in a moderate oven, sprinkle with powdered sugar and serve immediately.

APPLE SNOW.

Pare and core tart, juicy apples ; stew with just enough water to keep from burning ; sweeten with white sugar, and beat until perfectly free from lumps ; when cold, add the juice of half a lemon, and, for a dish large enough for eight or ten persons, the whites of two eggs ; beat the mixture until it is stiff enough to stand alone, and is as " white as snow," and you will have a delicious and elegant dessert ; eat with whipped cream.

CALEDONIAN CREAM.

Take two tablespoonfuls of raspberry jam, two of black currant jelly, and the whites of four eggs. Beat altogether for half an hour. A little powdered sugar may be added if desired, and there will be a delicious dish known as Caledonian cream.

APPLE MERINGUE.

Beat the yolks of three eggs well, and then beat with them a dish of apple sauce. Beat the whites of the eggs to a stiff froth, with two cups of sugar ; spread it over the apple sauce and set it in the oven for ten minutes. Peaches can be done in the same way, without the yolks of the eggs.

PUFFS FOR DINNER.

Two cups of flour, four eggs, two cups of milk, a pint of peaches, one cupful of sugar, one-half a cupful of butter. Beat the eggs thoroughly ; add the flour and milk by degrees. Fill custard cups about half full, and bake in a hot oven about ten minutes. Beat the peaches thoroughly with the butter and sugar, and use for a sauce to eat with the puffs, which must be served directly from the oven.

CREME A LA VALOIS.

Four sponge-cakes (small), three-quarters of a pint of cream, juice of half a lemon, one-quarter of a glass of pineapple juice (or substitute), one ounce and a quarter of isinglass, jam, sugar to taste. Cut the cakes into thin slices, place two together with jam or currant jelly between them, and pour over them a small quantity of pineapple juice. Sweeten and flavor the cream with the lemon-juice, add the isinglass, which should be dissolved in a little water, and beat up the cream well. Place a little in a mould, oiled with sweet oil, arrange the pieces of cake in the cream and fill the mould with the remainder ; let it cool and then turn out on a dish. By oiling the mould the cream will have a much smoother appearance, and will turn out more easily than when the mould is dipped in cold water.

PEACH CHARLOTTE.

Line the bottom and sides of a dish with slices of fresh sponge-cake. Pare some ripe peaches, cut them in halves, sprinkle sugar on them, and fill up the dish. Then whisk a pint of sweetened cream ; as the froth rises, take it off until all is done. Pile the cream on the top of the peaches and serve.

WHIPS.

Whites of three eggs, sugar to the taste, one pint of milk or cream. Stir the whites of the eggs (without beating them) into the milk. Add the sugar and whisk it to a froth, which must be taken off and put in glasses as it rises. Flavor with lemon or vanilla.

AN EXCELLENT TRIFLE.

Lay macaroons in the bottom of a pudding dish and cover with rich, cold-boiled custard. It must stand two or three inches deep. On that, place a layer of raspberry jam or currant jelly, and cover the whole very high with whipped cream, made the day before of rich cream, the whites of two well-beaten eggs, sugar and lemon-juice. If made the day before it is used, it has quite a different taste ; is solid and far better.

FLOATING ISLAND.

One quart of milk, sweetened ; four eggs, one tea-spoonful of extract of vanilla. Let the milk come to a boil, remove from the fire and add, a spoonful at a time, the yolks of the eggs, well beaten. When thick to the consistency of cream, flavor and pour into a glass dish. Have on the fire a shallow pan of hot water. Beat the whites of the eggs stiff, with two or three tablespoonfuls of powdered sugar, flavor slightly, and drop with a spoon into the pan of boiling water. Let each spoonful, after it is cooked, cool a moment, and then pile it on the soft custard in a glass dish.

CHOCOLATE BLANC MANGE.

One-half ounce of Cooper's gelatine, one quart of milk (scant), three-quarters of a cup of sugar, three eggs, four tablespoonfuls of grated chocolate, one teaspoonful and a half of extract of vanilla, one pint of whipped cream. Soak the gelatine, in a little cold water, one hour. Heat the milk to boiling, add the gelatine, stir until dissolved, then add the sugar and well-beaten yolks of eggs ; stir in the chocolate until wholly dissolved and smooth. Remove from the fire ; turn into a bowl and whip in lightly and briskly the beaten whites and vanilla. Pour into moulds wet with cold water.

SNOW PUDDING.

Half a box of Cox's gelatine, dissolved in one pint of boiling water. When almost cold, add one cup of sugar, juice of one lemon, one-half teaspoonful of lemon extract. Strain; add the whites of three beaten eggs. Beat all thoroughly together and pour it into a mould as it begins to thicken. Serve cold, with boiled custard made of the yolks of the eggs, half a teaspoonful corn starch, stirred into a pint of boiling milk, sweetened to taste; flavor with vanilla.

TAPIOCA CREAM.

After soaking three heaping tablespoonfuls of tapioca for an hour in water, boil it in a quart of milk, in a farina kettle, or in a tin pail set in a pot of boiling water. When the tapioca is cooked soft, stir in the yolks of four eggs, well beaten, with a cup of white sugar. Add a little salt, and keep stirring the tapioca for a few minutes. Have two of the whites ready to stir into the tapioca as soon as it is done. Flavor with vanilla, and pour into a pudding dish. Beat the other two whites to a stiff froth on a plate, and set the plate over a kettle of hot water. Let it stand a minute until it hardens; then cover the top of the pudding with it. To be eaten cold.

RICE SNOW CREAM.

Boil in a saucepan four ounces of ground rice, two ounces of butter, one quart of milk, for twenty minutes, or until the mixture is smooth. Flavor to taste. Pour into a buttered mould, and serve cold with sauce, or cream and sugar.

CREAM PUFFS.

One pint of water, one cup of butter, two cups flour, six eggs. Boil the water and butter together, then stir in the flour and set away to cool. When cool stir in the eggs, well beaten, and drop into pans, not too close together. Spread over them the white of one egg. When baked, open them on the side and fill with the following mixture: One egg, one cup of sugar, one tablespoonful of flour, one pint of boiling milk. Let all come to a boil, and cool before putting into the puffs.

GELATINE JELLY.

One box gelatine, one quart boiling water, two lemons. Soak the gelatine in a little cold water until soft. Add the boiling water, boiling five minutes, stirring constantly, also the juice of the lemon and a little of the grated rind. Strain until clear and pour into moulds.

SPANISH CREAM.

One-half box of gelatine, one quart of milk, four eggs, one cup and a half of sugar, lemon extract. Soak the gelatine in milk, after it is soft, set on the fire to boil. Beat the yolks of the eggs with one cup of sugar, beat light and stir into the boiling milk; remove from the fire while adding this. Stir well and return to the fire and cook until it thickens a little. Set away to cool. Beat the whites of the eggs, with the half cup of sugar, light and stiff, and add to the custard when cool; beat all well together; add the lemon to flavor. Put in moulds and serve with cream.

CHOCOLATE CREAM.

Four eggs, one-quarter pound of chocolate, one cup of sugar, one-half pint of hot water, one pint and one-half of cream. Beat the whites and yolks of the eggs separately, add the sugar to the yolks, then stir in the whites. Dissolve the chocolate in the hot water, and strain it; add the cream, let it boil once and pour it over the eggs, stirring all the time. Then put all into a pitcher, or small pail, setting that in boiling water, and stir until it thickens. To be served in glasses or custard cups and eaten cold.

VANILLA CREAM.

Three eggs, one-half pint of cream, one-half ounce of Cox's gelatine, one-half pint of milk, one tablespoonful of powdered sugar, one-half teaspoonful of essence of vanilla. Beat thoroughly the yolks of three eggs, and the white of one. Stir in the milk, and boil until it thickens. Then stand it aside to cool. Soak the gelatine in half a gill of cold water; then set it over the fire and stir until quite melted; strain it and pour it into the custard. Whip the cream to a froth, add the sugar and vanilla. When the custard is sufficiently cooled, stir it lightly into the whipped cream and pour the whole into a mould.

STRAWBERRY CREAM.

One pint of strawberries, two and one-half ounces of white sugar, one-half ounce of gelatine, one-half gill cold water, one-half pint of cream; juice of one lemon. Sprinkle half an ounce of the sugar over the strawberries, and pass them through a sieve. Soak the gelatine in the cold water, then set over the fire and stir until dissolved. Add the remainder of the sugar and lemon juice. Pass all this through a strainer, stir into the strawberries and mix well. Whip the cream to a stiff froth, add that, stir lightly and pour all into a mould.

CALVES' FOOT BLANC MANGE.

Boil four feet in five quarts of water, without any salt. When the liquor is reduced to one quart, strain it and mix with one quart of milk, and add several sticks of cinnamon or a vanilla bean. Boil the whole ten minutes, and sweeten it to taste with white sugar; strain it and fill your mould with it.

CURRANT, RASPBERRY, OR STRAWBERRY WHISK.

To three gills of the juice of the fruit add ten ounces of crushed sugar, the juice of a lemon, and one pint and one-half of cream. Whisk it until quite thick, and serve it in jelly glasses.

LEMON CREAM.

Beat one pint of thick, sweet cream until it is very light; then add the grated rind of one large lemon, the juice of two, and one-half pound of pulverized sugar. Serve this in wineglasses, or in small china cups.

AN ORNAMENTAL DISH.

Pare and core, without splitting, some small-sized apples, and boil them very gently with one lemon for every six apples. Make a syrup of half a pound of white sugar for each pound of apples. Boil the apples unbroken and the lemons sliced in the syrup, very gently until the apples look clear. Then take them up carefully, so as not to break them, and add to the syrup an ounce or more of gelatine, previously soaked ten or fifteen minutes in a little cold water and let it boil up. Strain the syrup and pour it over the apples after laying a slice of lemon on each one.

PEACH CREAM.

Cover with cold water half an ounce of Cox's gelatine, and let it stand ten or fifteen minutes. Then add a pint of cream and boil it. Have ready some canned peaches in a dish, and as the cream cools pour it over them.

RICE PEARS.

Boil a small cupful of rice in milk, mix two well-beaten eggs with it, and sweeten, flavoring it with orange or other jelly. Let it be quite thick, then make it up into the form of pears; dip them in a little batter made of egg and flour, sprinkle sifted sugar on them and set them in the oven until of a good brown. Stick a bit of citron in each for a stem, and serve with custard.

CHARLOTTE RUSSE.

One pint and one-fourth of milk; one pint of cream; one-half ounce of gelatine; slices of sponge cake or lady fingers; four eggs; vanilla. Set on the fire one pint of milk, and as it comes to a boil stir it into the well-beaten eggs; flavor, sweeten, and set it away to cool. Soak the gelatine in a gill of the cold milk, and then let it become warm, and when dissolved pour it into the cream and whip it thoroughly. When the custard is cold stir it into the cream. Transfer to a mould lined with the cake, and set it on ice.

OMELETTE SOUFFLE.

One cup of flour; one pint of milk; one spoonful of sugar; a small piece of butter; five eggs. Scald the milk, butter, and flour together. After the batter is cold, stir in the yolks of the eggs. Just before baking, mix in the whites very gently. Bake in a quick oven. Eat with sauce.

CAKE.

RULES FOR MAKING CAKE.

Have the ingredients all measured or weighed, and prepared, and the tins buttered before mixing the materials. Sift the cream of tartar, or baking powder with, and thoroughly mix it into the flour; dissolve the soda in the milk, or, if no milk is used, in a little warm (never hot) water; roll the sugar if lumpy; beat the butter and sugar to a cream; beat the yolks and whites of the eggs separately. When fruit is used, it must always be added the last thing, and dredged with flour to prevent its falling to the bottom. Cake, to be light, should be baked slowly at first, until the batter is evenly heated all through. Cake is very much more delicate if made with pulverized sugar than when made with the coarser granulated sugar. Eggs will beat lighter and quicker if they are placed in a basin of cold water for half an hour before using.

ICE CREAM CAKE.

Two cupfuls of sugar, one cupful of butter, three cupfuls of flour, one-half cupful of milk, and whites of eight eggs, one teaspoonful of cream tartar, one-half teaspoonful of soda, or in their place three teaspoonfuls of baking powder. Bake in thin cakes.

Icing.—Two and a half cups of powdered sugar, enough water to moisten, and boil. Beat the whites of three eggs to a stiff froth, and when the syrup is clear, pour it over the whites and stir very fast. Add half a teaspoonful of citric acid and flavor with vanilla.

WATERMELON CAKE.

One cupful and a half of sugar, half a cupful of butter, half a cupful of sour milk, two cupfuls of flour, whites of four eggs, half a teaspoonful of soda. Spread a thick layer of this cake in the bottom of the pan. Then take the same quantity of all the ingredients, using pink sugar instead of white, and the yolks of the eggs. Flavor with rose-water; add seedless raisins, and use for the middle of the cake. Then cover with another layer of first mixture.

IDA CAKE.

Six eggs, two teacupfuls of sugar, two teacupfuls of flour, one tablespoonful of melted butter, two teaspoonfuls of baking powder. Bake in jelly cake tins.

MOLLY CAKE.

Four eggs, three cupfuls of flour, two cupfuls of sugar, one cupful of milk, half a pound of butter, one teaspoonful of cream tartar, half a teaspoonful of soda.

MARBLE CAKE.

Two cupfuls of sugar, three cupfuls of flour (scant), three-quarters of a cupful of butter, four eggs, half a tumblerful of milk, half a teaspoonful of cream tartar, a quarter-teaspoonful of soda. MARBLE PART.—Two tablespoonfuls of molasses, one teaspoonful of allspice, one teaspoonful of cinnamon, one teaspoonful of nutmeg, a half-teaspoonful of cloves. Stir together the molasses and spices in a cup, fill up the cup with the cake ; put part of the cake in the pan, cover it with marble, and add the remainder of cake. Bake slowly.

JUMBLES.—NO. I.

One pound and a quarter of flour, one pound of butter, one pound of pulverized sugar, four eggs, one wine-glass of rose-water, half of a nutmeg. Cream the butter and sugar ; add the yolks, then the rose-water, next the flour and lastly the whites stirred in very lightly. Drop them into the pan with a spoon.

JUMBLES.—NO. II.

One pint of sour cream, two cups of sugar, three eggs, a quart of flour, into which is sifted two teaspoonfuls of baking powder ; season with cinnamon ; cut into rings and fry in lard to a light brown.

BRIDE'S CAKE.

Whites of six eggs beaten to a froth, two and one-half cups of sugar, one-half of a cup of butter, one-half of a cup of milk, two cups of flour, one teaspoonful of cream of tartar, half a teaspoonful of soda, flavor with rose.

CREAM CAKE.

Two cups of sugar, two cups of sour cream, four cups of flour, three eggs, one teaspoonful of soda, a little nutmeg.

PARK STREET CAKE.

Whites and yolks of four eggs, beaten separately, two cups of sugar, one cup of milk, three cups of flour, half a crp of butter, one teaspoonful of soda, two teaspoonfuls of cream tartar.

WHITE MOUNTAIN CAKE.

Eight eggs, reserving the whites of three for icing ; one coffeecup of butter, two of sugar, half a cup of milk, one teaspoonful of soda, two teaspoonfuls of cream tartar, the rind and juice of one lemon, a little nutmeg, a full pint of flour, measured before sifting. Cream the butter and sugar ; add the yolks, lemon, spice, milk, white of eggs, and lastly the flour. Bake in jelly-cake pans. Make the icing with one pound of pulverized sugar, flavored with vanilla, and spread it between the cakes. This quantity makes two cakes of three layers each.

ALMOND CAKE.

One pound of sugar, half a pound of butter, one cup of milk, six eggs, one pound of flour, three teaspoonfuls of Royal baking powder, one teaspoonful of essence of almonds. Beat the yolks of the eggs and the sugar perfectly light, then add the butter and beat again ; then the flour and milk ; lastly, the whites of eggs, well beaten.

GRANDMOTHER'S CAKE.

Two-thirds of a cup of butter, two cups of sugar, three cups of flour, half a cupful of sweet milk, four eggs, one teaspoonful of cream tartar, one-half teaspoonful of soda, one cup of stoned raisins. Citron and lemon-peel to taste.

ORANGE CAKE.—NO. I.

One cup and a half of sugar, two-thirds of a cup of butter, two and a half cups of flour, two teaspoonfuls of cream tartar, one teaspoonful of soda, a small cup of milk, the yolks of five eggs. Bake in four jelly-cake pans.

ORANGE CAKE.—NO. II.

Two cups each of sugar and flour, half a cupful of water, the yolks of five eggs, the juice and rind of one lemon, half a teaspoonful of soda, one teaspoonful of cream tartar. Bake in jelly-cake pans.

CUSTARD FOR ORANGE CAKE. — Beat the whites of
the eggs to a stiff froth, add one cupful of powdered
sugar, the grated rind and juice of one lemon and one
orange. Beat until as thick as cream.

NELLIE'S SPONGE CAKE.

Six eggs beaten two minutes, add three cupfuls of
sugar and beat five minutes, then add two cupfuls of
flour with two teaspoonfuls of cream tartar, and beat two
minutes. One cup of cold water with one teaspoonful of
soda dissolved in it and two cupfuls more of flour. The
rind of one lemon and half of the juice ; a little salt.
Bake in a moderate oven.

SPONGE CAKE.—NO. I.

Ten eggs, one pound of pulverized sugar, a half-pound
of flour, juice of half a large lemon, with the grated rind.
After all the ingredients are quite ready—i. e., the flour
and sugar sifted, the lemon-peel grated, the half lemon
squeezed, and the tins buttered—the success of this cake
is in the beating of the eggs. Two persons should beat
them at least half an hour, one beating the whites and
the other the yolks and half the sugar together. Then
stir in lightly the remainder of the sugar, finally the
flour and lemon by degrees.

SPONGE CAKE.—NO. II.

Three eggs, one cup of flour, one cup of sugar, one
teaspoonful of cream tartar, one-quarter of a teaspoonful
of soda, one teaspoonful and a half of lemon. First beat
the eggs to a froth, then add the sugar. Mix the cream
tartar in the flour and add the lemon. Dissolve the soda
in a tablespoonful of warm water, and add last.

SPONGE CAKE.—NO. ·III.

Two cups of sugar, two cups of flour, half a cup of
milk, six eggs, one lemon, two teaspoonfuls of cream
tartar, one teaspoonful of soda.

BERWICK SPONGE CAKE.

Six eggs, three cupfuls of sugar, two cupfuls of flour, one cupful of water, one teaspoonful of soda, two more cupfuls of flour, in which is thoroughly mixed two teaspoonfuls of cream tartar. A little salt, the rind of a lemon and a tablespoonful of the juice.

GUSSIE'S SPONGE CAKE.

One cupful of sugar, five eggs, one cupful of flour, one teaspoonful of vinegar. Beat the yolks and sugar ; add the beaten whites, then the flour and vinegar.

EXCELLENT SPONGE CAKE.

Ten eggs, their weight in sugar, the weight of six eggs in flour. Beat the yolks and sugar together until very light ; beat the whites separately, then add them to the yolks and sugar with the grated rind of one lemon and the juice of two. Stir in the flour lightly, when ready to go into the oven.

CRULLERS.

Five eggs, half a cupful of sugar. Beat well together and add one teacupful of cream or milk. A piece of butter as large as two eggs, half a teaspoonful of soda, two teaspoonfuls of cream tartar. A little cinnamon or nutmeg. Flour sufficient to make a dough that will roll out. Fry in hot lard.

DOUGHNUTS.

One coffeecup each of sugar and of milk, two eggs, one teaspoonful of soda, two teaspoonfuls of cream tartar.

ESSEX CAKE.

Five eggs, three cupfuls of sugar, one cupful of butter, one cupful of sour milk, four cupfuls of flour, one teaspoonful of soda, cloves, cinnamon, nutmeg and raisins.

FEATHER CAKE.

Two cupfuls of powdered sugar, three eggs, half a cupful of butter, one cupful of milk, three teaspoonfuls of baking powder with three cupfuls of flour. Flavor with vanilla.

COMPOSITION CAKE.

Three cupfuls of sugar, two cupfuls of butter, four cupfuls of flour (full), one cupful of milk, six eggs, two teaspoonfuls of cream tartar, one teaspoonful of soda, one pound of raisins, spice to the taste.

. TEA CAKE.

One small cupful of butter, three cupfuls of sugar, four and a half cupfuls of flour, four eggs, one teaspoonful of soda, two teaspoonfuls of cream tartar.

HUCKLEBERRY CAKE.

Half a cupful of butter, two cupfuls of sugar, one egg, one cupful of milk, one teaspoonful of soda, one teaspoonful of cream tartar, one pint of huckleberries. Very nice if eaten warm.

BLUEBERRY CAKE.

Two cupfuls of milk, three eggs, one cupful and a half of sugar, two tablespoonfuls of melted butter, three teaspoonfuls of cream tartar, one teaspoonful and a half of soda, berries, flour.

NUT CAKE.

One cupful of raisins, one cupful of walnuts, one cupful of sugar, half a cupful of butter, half a cupful of milk, two cups of flour, two eggs, one teaspoonful of cream tartar, half a teaspoonful of soda.

COCOANUT CAKE.

One pound of sugar, one pound of flour, half a pound of butter, six eggs, one small cup of sweet milk, one teaspoonful of soda, two teaspoonfuls of cream tartar. Bake in thin cakes.

ICING—Whites of four eggs beaten to a froth ; stir in sugar until thick enough.   Spread this on each cake and sprinkle grated cocoanut over it.

COCOANUT CONES.

Two large cocoanuts, grated, whites of three eggs, well beaten, half a pound of pulverized sugar, a quarter of a teaspoonful of vanilla. Make into cones, cover with well-buttered white paper ; bake on an inverted pan in a quick oven from twenty to thirty minutes.

GOLDEN CAKE.

Two cups of sugar, one cup of butter, one large cup of milk, three cups of flour, one teaspoonful of cream tartar, half a teaspoonful of soda.

LEMON CAKE.

Three cups of sugar, four cups of flour, five eggs, one cup of milk, one cup of butter, juice of one lemon, the rind grated in, half a teaspoonful of soda, a little salt.

JELLY CAKE.

Two cups of sugar, three-quarters of a cup of butter, one cup of sweet milk, four cups of flour, three eggs, one teaspoonful of soda, two teaspoonfuls of cream tartar. Flavor with lemon or whatever is liked.

FRENCH JUMBLES.

Half a pound of flour, one pound of sugar, three-quarters of a pound of butter, three eggs.   Dissolve one teaspoonful of soda in half a cup of milk ; add this, and one nutmeg.   Roll out the dough and cut it into small cakes and bake in a quick oven.

JUMBLES.—NO. II.

One pound and a half of flour, three-quarters of a

pound each of butter and of sugar, four eggs. A little nutmeg. Make into small cakes.

FRUIT CAKE.

Half a pound of butter, half a pound of citron, one pound of raisins, one pound of currants, two cups of sugar, three cups of flour, one tablespoonful of molasses, one tablespoonful of cinnamon, four eggs, one nutmeg, a little soda. Bake from three to four hours in a slow oven.

WHITE FRUIT CAKE.

One cup of butter and two cups of white sugar, well beaten together; one cup of milk, two and a half cups of flour, and the whites of seven eggs; two even spoonfuls of baking-powder; beat all well before adding fruit. One pound each of raisins, figs, dates and blanched almonds, and one quarter of a pound of citron; cut all fine. Stir the fruit in last with a sifting of flour over it. Bake slowly.

FRUIT CAKE.

Two cupfuls each of molasses and brown sugar, one cup of sweet milk, two cups of butter, five cups of flour, five eggs, one teaspoonful of soda, two teaspoonfuls of cream tartar, one pound each of raisins and currants, half a pound of citron, spice to taste. Add the fruit, having floured it, the last thing.

TUMBLER CAKE.

One tumbler each of sugar, butter, molasses and sweet milk; four tumblerfuls of flour, one tumblerful each of sliced citron and raisins, or currants, one teaspoonful each of cinnamon, nutmeg, cloves and soda, two teaspoonfuls of cream tartar, four eggs. This makes two loaves.

JELLY ROLLS.

Three eggs, half a cupful of butter, one cup of flour, two-thirds of a cup of pulverized sugar, one teaspoonful

94 THE MODEL COOK.

and a half of baking powder, a little salt. Bake in well-buttered pans in which the dough is to be about half an inch thick. Take it carefully from the tins when baked, and lay it on a cloth ; spread jelly over it evenly with a knife, and roll while hot or the cake will crumble.

SAND TARTS.

Ten ounces of butter, one pound of sifted sugar, one pound of flour, two eggs. Rub the butter into the flour, add the sugar, then the eggs, well beaten ; roll out. Then beat up one egg and rub a little over each cake, and afterwards sift sugar and ground cinnamon mixed together over them. Bake.

COOKIES.

One cup each of butter and sugar, two eggs, and enough flour to roll out. Roll very thin, and bake only ten or fifteen minutes.

COOKIES.

One cup and one-third of butter, two cups of sugar, half a cup of sweet milk, one teaspoonful of soda, two teaspoonfuls of cream tartar, two eggs, one nutmeg.

SOFT COOKIES.

Two cups of sugar, one cup each of butter and sour milk, three and a half cups of flour, two eggs, half a teaspoonful of soda. Spread thin on buttered pans ; sift sugar over them and bake.

GINGER POUND CAKE.

Three-quarters of a pound of melted butter, one pound of sifted flour, one cup of brown sugar, one pint of New Orleans molasses, five eggs, two teaspoonfuls of cinnamon, one small teaspoonful of soda mixed in a little milk.

MOLASSES DROP CAKE.

Two cups of molasses, one cup of butter, half a cup of hot water, two eggs, two teaspoonfuls of soda, three teaspoonfuls of ginger, one teaspoonful of cinnamon, one teaspoonful of cloves, flour to make as stiff as loaf cake. Drop on tins and bake.

GINGERBREAD.

One pound and a half of flour, half a pound of butter, half a pound of brown sugar, one pint of molasses, one ounce each of ginger and cinnamon, one teaspoonful and a half of allspice, half a teaspoonful of cloves, one teaspoonful of soda, dissolved in a little milk. Add the soda last, and set the mixture aside for the night. Bake in the morning.

COMMON GINGERBREAD.

One quart of flour, one teacupful of butter, two teacupfuls of sugar, three teacupfuls of molasses, one teacupful of milk, one teaspoonful of soda, two teaspoonfuls of cream tartar. Spice to taste.

MRS. E.'S GINGERBREAD.

Half a cup of butter, three cups of flour, one cup of boiling water, one teaspoonful of soda, two teaspoonfuls of cream tartar, one tablespoonful of ginger.

LULU'S GINGERBREAD.

One cup each of sugar, molasses and butter, three eggs, one tablespoonful of soda dissolved in one cup of blood-warm water, three cups of flour. Spice to the taste. Bake in a slow oven.

RICH SMALL CAKES.

Three eggs, three tablespoonfuls each of butter and sugar, three cups of flour, one teaspoonful of essence of lemon, half a nutmeg. Cream the butter and sugar, add the other ingredients, beat well together, roll out thin, and cut into small cakes.

CHOCOLATE CAKE.

Two cups of powdered sugar, half a cupful of butter, one cup of milk, three cups of flour, three eggs, one teaspoonful of soda, two teaspoonfuls of cream tartar. Bake as for jelly-cake.

Filling.—One-quarter of a cake of chocolate, one-half of a cup of sweet milk, one tablespoonful of corn starch, one teaspoonful of vanilla. Mix these ingredients together with the exception of the vanilla; boil two minutes, flavor and then sweeten to the taste, and spread thickly between the layers of cake.

QUEEN'S CAKE.

One cup of butter, two cups of sugar, one cup of milk, four cups of flour, five eggs, one teaspoonful of soda, two teaspoonfuls of cream tartar.

WEDDING CAKE.

Four pounds each of flour and sugar, three pounds of butter, five pounds of raisins, three pounds of currants, forty eggs, one ounce of mace, half an ounce of nutmeg, six teaspoonfuls of rose water, four teaspoonfuls of cream tartar, two teaspoonfuls of soda.

SIMPLE TEA CAKE.

One teacupful of sugar, half a teacupful of butter, one teacupful of milk, half a teaspoonful of soda, one teaspoonful of cream tartar. Enough flour to roll it out. Cut in thin cakes.

CUP CAKE.

One cup of butter, two cups of sugar, three cups of flour, four eggs, one teaspoonful of soda, two teaspoonfuls of cream tartar. Nutmeg.

DELICATE CAKE.

One cup of butter, two cups of sugar, three cups of flour, half a cupful of milk, the whites of five eggs, one teaspoonful of soda. A little nutmeg.

SILVER CAKE.

One cupful of sugar, two cupfuls of flour, half a cupful each of butter and milk, half a teaspoonful of soda, one teaspoonful of cream tartar, the whites of four eggs.

CHOCOLATE FROSTING.

One cup of brown sugar, one cup of grated chocolate, half a cup of water. Boil until thick, and spread on cake while hot.

WHITE FROSTING.

Cover with hot water as much gelatine as can be taken up in the two fingers, set it on the stove in a pan of hot water until dissolved, and stir into it a cup of white sugar. Flavor with lemon.

ICING FOR CAKES.

Beat up well the white of an egg, mix with it, by degrees, three ounces of powdered sugar, and cover the cake with it. Set it in a cold place until quite firm. To ornament it, take some of the same mixture, and color it pink with beet-root juice, or red currant jelly. To apply the pink icing, twist a piece of writing paper in the form of a cone, half fill it with the frosting, taking care to leave a small hole at the point for the icing to run through. Fold the large end of the cone securely. By a gentle, careful squeezing, the icing may be forced out of the point of the cone in a small stream, and by properly directing this stream, various ornamental figures may be formed.

PRESERVES, CANNED FRUITS, JELLIES, ETC.

PRESERVED PUMPKIN.

Cut a thick, yellow pumpkin into strips about two inches wide and five inches long. Add a pound of white sugar to each pound of pumpkin, and two wineglassfuls of lemon juice. The next day, add the parings of one or two lemons to the sugared pumpkin and boil the whole three-quarters of an hour, or long enough to make the syrup clear without breaking the slices. Take out the pumpkin to cool ; strain the syrup, and pour over it.

BLACKBERRY JAM.

To each pound of ripe fruit (very ripe), stewed in a procelain kettle, add one pound of best loaf sugar, mashing all together thoroughly with a strong wooden spoon, while still upon the fire. When well mixed and boiled fifteen minutes longer, stirring well the meanwhile, fill small jars or glasses, and set away. The jam made of blackberries is particularly useful in dysentery, and similar complaints.

PRESERVED PEARS.

Peel two dozen Bartlett pears and cut them into halves or not, as preferred. Soak them in boiling water for ten minutes, then pour clarified syrup of white sugar over them, and boil them for a short time.

PRESERVED PINEAPPLES.

To one pound of pineapple allow one pound of white sugar. Slice the fruit and let it stand in the sugar over night. In the morning take out the pineapple, and set the syrup on the fire until it begins to simmer. A piece of ginger root boiled with the syrup will add to the flavor of the preserve. When the syrup is hot, add the fruit and boil ten or fifteen minutes, and afterward boil the syrup alone, and pour it over the pineapple.

PRESERVED QUINCES.

After washing and wiping the fruit thoroughly, pare and core it, saving the skins and cores for jelly. Then cut the quinces into halves or quarters, according to size. Allow a pound of sugar, and a teacupful of water to each pound of fruit. Put the sugar and water in the kettle and boil and skim till no scum arises. Then add the fruit, and let it boil for about an hour and a half, or until it looks clear. It should always boil hard.

CANNED PEACHES.

To three pounds of the fruit allow one pound of sugar and two cupfuls of water. Set the water and sugar over the fire, and as it comes to a boil add the peaches with the stones, as they give a fine flavor to the fruit. If the peaches are very ripe, they will only need to be heated through thoroughly. In the meantime have ready a deep pan of hot water, in which stand the jars with hot water in them. Turn the hot water out of the jars and fill them with the fruit and syrup, so full that a little of the latter escapes. Have the lid hot, and clap it on the overflowing jar, and screw down, giving it a final twist when cold.

CANNED PEACHES.—NO. II.

Have one porcelain kettle with boiling water, and another with a syrup made sweet enough with white sugar for the peaches ; pare, halve, and drop the peaches into the boiling water ; let them remain until a silver fork will pierce them ; lift them out with a wire spoon, fill the can, pour in all the boiling syrup the can will hold and seal immediately. (The can must be made hot before the peaches are put in.) Continue in this way, preparing and sealing only one can at a time until done.

CANNED PINEAPPLE.

After paring the pineapple and removing the eyes, cut it into slices. Allow half a pound of sugar to a pound of fruit, sprinkling the sugar over the slices and letting them stand all night. In the morning fill the cans with fruit and syrup, place on the tops very loosely, and set them in a deep kettle full of water, so that only the necks of the jars are above it. Let the water boil for twenty minutes and then screw down the tops. Place a piece of board in the bottom of the kettle to keep the jars from direct contact with it.

CANNED PEARS.

Bartlett or Seckel pears are especially good for this purpose. Peel them, leaving the stems on. Make a syrup of one pound of sugar and two cups of water to three pounds of pears. Let the pears boil a few minutes until tender. When filling the jars, allow a little of the syrup to run over to make sure that they are quite full.

CIDER JELLY.

A delicious jelly can be made of cider. To one pint of clear, sweet cider, allow one pint of cold water, two pounds of sugar, one package of gelatine, one large pint of boiling water. Soak the gelatine in the cold water, and heat until it is entirely dissolved, then add to this the sugar, a spoonful of cinnamon, the juice of two lemons, the grated rind of two, then the dissolved gelatine. Add the cider last, then turn all into a thick flannel bag, and let it drain. Do not squeeze the bag at all. Pour the clear liquid into bowls or glasses and set away to cool.

BLACKBERRY JELLY.

Bruise the fruit, put in a thin cloth, and allow it to strain over night. Next morning add half a pound of sugar to each pint of juice; boil twenty minutes.

APPLE JELLY.—NO. I.

Pare the apples and cut them up, removing the cores. To a pound of apple add three ounces of sugar, half a pint of water and the juice and grated rind of one lemon; cook until tender. Dissolve one ounce of gelatine in half a gill of water, and when the apples are thoroughly cooked and rubbed through a sieve stir the gelatine into them. Rinse the mould in cold water, pour in the jelly and set aside to cool. After the jelly is turned out, place one-half of a pint of whipped cream around it on the dish.

APPLE JELLY.—NO. II.

To thirteen good-sized apples, add one quart of water and one lemon; boil until soft, and strain. To one pint of juice add one pound of sugar, and boil twenty minutes.

LEMON JELLY.

To the juice, pulp and grated rind of three lemons add one pound and a half of sugar. To a quart of boiling water add one ounce of Cox's gelatine; when it is dissolved add the other ingredients and the whites of four eggs, well beaten. Let it all boil up once, and then turn into moulds.

RED CURRANT JELLY.

Wash the currants, and drain them; mash them with the back of a spoon; put them in a jelly bag, and squeeze until all the juice is pressed out; to every pint of juice allow a pound of loaf sugar; boil the juice and the sugar twenty minutes, skimming all the while; pour it warm into the glasses, and when cold, tie it up with brandied paper. Jellies should never be allowed to get cold in the kettle; if boiled too long, they will lose their flavor and become of a dark color. Strawberry, raspberry, blackberry and grape jelly may be made in the same manner, and with the same proportion of loaf sugar.

MRS. T.'S CURRANT JELLY.

Mash the currants and throw them, stems and all, into a kettle ; boil ten or fifteen minutes. Strain them, and boil the juice again ten or fifteen minutes ; then, while hot, stir in one pound of sugar for every pint of juice, and in a few minutes the jelly will come.

QUINCE JELLY.

When making quince preserves, use the skins and cores for jelly, of course adding as many quinces as may be convenient. Boil until tender in as much water as will cover them. Then strain through a sieve, but do not press the fruit. Afterward pass the juice through a jelly bag, and add a pound of white sugar to each pint of juice. When the sugar is dissolved, set it where it will boil, and skim until a jelly is formed, which can be decided by dropping a small quantity into a tumbler of cold water.

PEACH PICKLE.

Seven pounds of fruit, three pounds of brown sugar, one quart of vinegar, one handful of whole cloves, two handfuls of whole cinnamon. Heat the vinegar, sugar and spices to boiling, and add as many peaches as will cook easily. Let them cook slowly until soft, but not enough to fall to pieces. Place them in jars, and add more peaches to the syrup until all are cooked.

SPICED CURRANTS.

Five pounds of ripe currants, four pounds of brown sugar, two tablespoonfuls of cloves, two of cinnamon, one pint of vinegar. Boil until thick.

SPICED GRAPES.

Four quarts of grapes, stoned, six pounds of sugar, one tablespoonful of allspice, one tablespoonful of cinnamon, and one of cloves, one pint of good vinegar. Cook several hours over a slow fire.

CANTALOUPE PICKLES.

Five pounds of cantaloupes, pared and sliced in the creases; put over them two pounds of sugar, and let them stand over night. Then pour off the syrup, and add one quart of vinegar, half an ounce each of cinnamon, cloves and mace, tied in cloths ; boil and skim ; add the cantaloupe, and boil fifteen minutes ; skim out and boil four or five hours, or until thick, then pour over the cantaloupes.

LEMON BUTTER.

Two lemons, two cups of sugar, four eggs, a piece of butter size of a hickory-nut. Beat the eggs together ; stir in the sugar and lemons, grating the rind, and squeezing the juice. Cook in a farina-kettle until thick. It will become thicker after cooling.

GRAPE BUTTER.

One peck of fox grapes, stew and strain through a colander, then put back into the kettle. Stew a quarter of a peck of sour apples, and pass through the colander, and add them to the grapes. Add five pounds of sugar, or sweeten to taste. Stir constantly. Make a little thinner than apple-butter.

TOMATO BUTTER.

Ten pounds of tomatoes, skinned and seeded, four pounds of sugar, one quart of vinegar, spiced with cloves, allspice and cinnamon, one tablespoonful each.

STEWED OR BAKED FRUIT.

BAKED APPLES.

Hollow out six apples ; set them on a pan each on a piece of plain paper ; fill each with thick cream, sprinkle sugar over them and bake slowly.

BOILED APPLES.

Peel six or eight large apples, and after making a thin syrup of half a pound of sugar to a quart of water, boil them in it slowly until tender. Add water if the syrup boils away too fast.

STEWED APPLES.

Cut the apples in halves and carefully peel them, leaving a thin bar of the skin across the center. Place core downward in a shallow pan of boiling water and cook until tender ; then carefully remove to a glass dish without breaking. Let the syrup come to a boil, sweeten, and thicken with a little gelatine ; flavor with lemon or vanilla, and when about to become a jelly, pour over the apples ; set away to cool. Before serving, beat up the whites of two eggs and two tablespoonfuls of powdered sugar, and spread on the top. The little trouble required to make this dish will be amply repaid by its beauty and excellence.

STEWED PRUNES.

Wash quickly in cold water to remove the grit, a pound and a half of prunes ; if very fresh and moist, this will not be necessary. Put them into a pudding-basin with a quarter of a pound of sugar and enough cold water to cover them ; cover the dish with a plate, and set it in a moderate oven, to remain there until the prunes are sufficiently done for the stones to be easily pressed out of them, which must be ascertained by trying them from time to time with a silver fork.

CANDIED OR GLACÈ FRUIT.

One pound of white sugar, and as little water as possible ; let it boil down, and skim it until it is perfectly clear and thick ; whatever fruit you desire to candy dip piece by piece into the hot syrup, and then spread them on a dish and they will soon become hard.

SNOWED FRUIT.

Professor Blot gives this recipe : The white of one egg, beaten well with a little water ; dip the fruit in the egg, and roll it immediately in granulated sugar. Place it on a dish and let it stand five or six hours ; small fruits, cherries and currants, are delicious prepared in this way.

CANDY.

CHOCOLATE CARAMELS.

One teacupful each of molasses, milk, white sugar and brown sugar, a quarter of a cup of butter, one tablespoonful of flour mixed in the milk, one teaspoonful of vanilla when nearly done, half a pound of chocolate. Boil twenty minutes.

BUTTER TAFFY.

Two cups of brown sugar, two cups of hot water, one tablespoonful of butter, put in slowly after it commences to boil.

COCOANUT CANDY.

Grate a cocoanut, and having ready two pounds of finely-sifted sugar, and the beaten whites of two eggs, also the milk of the nut, mix altogether and make into little cakes. In a short time the candy will be dry enough to eat.

ICE CREAM.

FLORENCE'S ICE CREAM.

Two quarts of milk, salted, six eggs, two cups of sugar. Let it come to a boil. When cold add one pint of cream and vanilla to flavor.

LEMON OR ORANGE ICE CREAM.

Squeeze a dozen lemons or oranges, and make the juice thick with sugar ; then stir in slowly three quarts of cream and freeze it.

CHOCOLATE, TEA AND COFFEE.

PLAIN CHOCOLATE.

Scrape one ounce (one of the small squares) of Baker's or any plain chocolate, fine ; add to this two tablespoonfuls of sugar, and put into a small saucepan with one tablespoonful of hot water ; stir over a hot fire for a minute or two, until it is perfectly smooth and glossy ; then stir it all into a quart of boiling milk, or half milk and half water ; mix thoroughly and serve immediately. If the beverage is desired richer, take twice as much chocolate, sugar and water. Made in this way, chocolate is perfectly smooth and free from oily particles. If it is allowed to boil after the chocolate is added to the milk, it becomes oily and loses its fine flavor.—*Maria Parloa.*

COFFEE.

We have tried all sorts of inventions for making good coffee, and have invariably returned to the old method, which is this : Grind the coffee just before making it ;

mix it thoroughly in a bowl with a little water and one egg slightly beaten. Scald the coffeepot with boiling water just before putting in the coffee. Let it boil hard fifteen minutes, then put it aside to settle. Pour off carefully into the urn or coffeepot. Use with it on the table plenty of hot milk and a teaspoonful or two of cream to each cup. Very few people realize the advantage of hot milk. Try it.

TO MAKE TEA.

Have the teakettle boiling when the teapot is scalded ; put in the tea immediately after scalding the pot. Black and green tea mixed is a favorite. Set it where it will keep hot but not boil, as all experienced housekeepers know how ruinous boiling is to tea. Lump sugar is the best for coffee and tea, but of course any will do.

BLACKBERRY DRINK.

To twelve quarts of the berries add two quarts of clear water, with five ounces of tartaric acid dissolved in it. Let this stand forty-eight hours ; then let the juice drip through a flannel cloth or sieve without pressure. To a pint of this juice add a pound of sugar and bottle forthwith. Tie over the mouth of each bottle a piece of cloth, and let it stand about ten days. Then cork the bottles and use when desired, remembering the acid liquid is never used alone, but diluted with two-thirds of its quantity of ice water. The juice of strawberries, raspberries, currants or Morello cherries may be prepared in the same way.

FOR THE SICK ROOM.

FOR A COUGH.

Take a tablespoonful of Iceland moss, dissolve it, and beat it up well in a glass of very hot water. Then strain it ; add a little sugar and lemon, and take a teaspoonful of it every little while.

WINE WHEY.

To half a pint of boiling milk add one-half the quantity of sherry wine, with constant stirring. Then strain and add two teaspoonfuls of sugar, and nutmeg to the taste.

SOUP FOR AN INVALID.

Cut in small pieces one pound of beef or mutton, or a part of both ; boil it gently in two quarts of water ; take off the scum, and when reduced to a pint, strain it. Season with a little salt, and take a teacupful at a time.

TOAST WATER.

Cut a slice, half an inch thick, of stale bread, remove the crust and toast on both sides. Place the toast and a piece of orange or lemon peel in a suitable vessel, add a pint of boiling water, cover, strain when cold. An agreeable drink in fever.

RAW MEAT.

Make a not very thick broth of tapioca and let it cool. Dilute finely scraped meat with cold soup till it resembles tomato soup. Add the tapioca with constant stirring.

INVALID'S COFFEE.

Add a large spoonful of coffee to a pint of milk. As it begins to boil, let it stand on the corner of the range for fifteen minutes, then sprinkle into it a little gelatine ; let it come to the boiling point again, after which set it back to settle. When thoroughly settled, pour it off carefully and sweeten with pulverized rock candy. Prepared in this way it is invaluable for persons with weak lungs.

EGG NOG.

One egg, two teaspoonfuls of white sugar, one tablespoonful of sherry wine, two tablespoonfuls each of cream or rich milk and water, grated nutmeg to taste. Beat the yolk to a froth and mix with the other ingredients, then add the white, beaten to a froth in a separate vessel.

BEEF EXTRACT.

Soak finely-chopped lean meat in an equal weight of cold water for an hour, then gradually raise to boiling point. Simmer for fifteen minutes. Press and strain. Add a little salt.

BLACKBERRY CORDIAL.

Four quarts of blackberries, one quart of cold water, six pounds of sugar. Place over night in a stone jar, well covered. In the morning boil gently for twenty minutes. When sufficiently cool, strain the juice through a flannel bag, and add two ounces of the essence of cloves, one ounce of whole allspice, one quart of Jamaica rum. Bottle when cool, and seal tightly. This recipe is invaluable for summer complaints.

EXCELLENT COUGH SYRUP.

One ounce of the herb thoroughwort, one ounce of slippery-elm bark, one ounce of whole flaxseed. Boil or soak in one quart of water. Strain and add one ounce of liquorice, one pint of the best molasses, one-half pound of loaf sugar. Boil thirty minutes, bottle and take three doses daily.

SUNDRIES.

BENZINE FOR CLEANING CLOTHING.

Benzine, applied with perseverance, is an effective agent in removing oil and tar spots from clothing.

TO CLEAN MARBLE.

Two parts common soda, one part pumice-stone, one part of finely powdered chalk. Sift through a fine sieve, and then mix with water. Rub the mixture over the marble, and then wash the marble with soap and water, and the stains will be removed.

TO MAKE WHITEWASH SMOOTH.

Put in a piece of washing soap about the size of two fingers. This will also keep the whitewash from rubbing off.

BLACKING STOVES.

In blacking stoves try greasing them with fresh grease before blacking. It prevents them from rusting. Add a pinch of brown sugar to blacking just before applying. This causes it to stick, and it polishes much easier, and with half the usual rubbing.

USES OF AMMONIA.

Housekeepers may be glad to know that a tablespoonful of ammonia in one gallon of warm water will restore the color of carpets. The pantry shelves are getting grimy, or finger-marks around the door-latches and knobs are looking dark and unsightly. For lack of time they are left day after day, for it is hard work to scour all the time, and it wears off the paint, too. Now suppose the wife has her bottle of spirits of ammonia to use; she takes her basin of water and a clean cloth, just puts on a few drops of the fluid, and wipes off all the dirt; it is worth more than half a day's labor, and does not hurt the paint, either. She could put a few drops in her dish water, and see how easily the dishes could be cleaned ; a few drops on a sponge would clean all the windows in the sitting room, making them shine like crystal. It would take the stains off the teaspoons, and a teaspoonful in the mop-pail would do more in washing up the kitchen floor than ten pounds of elbow grease applied to the mop-handle. A housewife has just as much right to make her work easy and expeditious as her husband has. If she does not do it, the fault is her own in a great measure.

FLAT IRONS.

If your flat irons are rough and smoky, lay a little fine salt on a flat surface and rub them well. It will prevent them from sticking to anything starched, and make them smooth.

CELERY SALT.

Save the root of the celery plant, dry and grate it, mixing it with one-third as much salt. Kept in a bottle well corked, it is delicious for soups, oysters, gravies or hashes.

THINGS WORTH KNOWING.

1. That fish may be scaled much easier by first dipping them into boiling water for about a minute.

2. That fish may be well scaled, if desired, before packing down in salt, though in that case do not scald them.

3. That salt fish are quickest and best freshened by soaking in sour milk.

4. That milk which is slightly turned or changed, may be sweetened and rendered fit for use again by stirring in a little soda.

5. That salt will curdle new milk ; hence, in preparing milk porridge, gravies, etc., the salt should not be added until the dish is prepared.

6. That fresh meat, after beginning to sour, will sweeten if placed out of doors, in the cool air, over night.

7. That clear, boiling water will remove tea stains and many fruit stains. Pour the water through the stain and thus prevent its spreading over the fabric.

8. That ripe tomatoes will remove ink and other stains from white cloth ; also from the hands.

9. That a tablespoonful of turpentine boiled with your white clothes will greatly aid the whitening process.

10. That boiled starch is much improved by the addition of a little spermaceti, or a little salt, or both, or a little gum arabic, dissolved.

11. That beeswax and salt will make your rusty flat-irons as clean and smooth as glass. Tie a lump of wax in a rag, and keep it for the purpose. When the irons are hot, rub them first with the wax rag, then scour with a paper, or cloth sprinkled with salt.

12. That kerosene will soften boots or shoes which have been hardened by water, and render them as pliable as new.

13. That kerosene will make your tin tea-kettle as bright as new. Saturate a woolen rag and rub with it.

To wash chamois skins, use cold water with plenty of soap, and rinse well in clear, cold water ; thus treated, the skins will never be hard, but soft and pliable.

A good coat of lime whitewash will destroy mold in cellars.

TABLE DECORATIONS.

When the whole world seems to have gone mad on the subject of decoration, perhaps a few hints would not be out of place here, especially for those who live in retired places, remote from the cities, and have not the opportunities of seeing and discussing new things.

Even those who have a hard, busy life, with multitudes of cares and very little money, can to some extent train their children to a love for the beautiful that will never leave them. The woods are full of lovely things for decoration, and we shall not soon forget the large, shallow dish of red bunch-berries, in their deep green leaves; that graced a certain table and elicited general admiration.

On a breakfast, dinner or tea-table, a large bowl of flowers looks very attractive, even though the flowers are common petunias or phloxes, or sweet peas, so often seen in the yard of farmhouses, and now when wild flowers are so popular, what can be more graceful or glowing than a vase of golden-rod and purple asters ? In the absence of showy flowers of any kind, wild or cultivated, in one's vicinity, gather grasses and make a bouquet of them ; their misty, waving heads will give the children something to think of besides the potatoes and pork and beans they swallow in such a hurry.

A city table to which a dozen gentlemen sat down was decorated with a strip of crimson plush about a quarter of a yard in width, bordered on either side with white daisies. Another, arranged for a party of six gentlemen, was a perfect bank of flowers, only a narrow strip on either side being reserved for the plates.

Whatever the decorations, whether cheap or expensive, with care and thought they can be made valuable, especially at home.

BILLS OF FARE FOR EACH DAY IN THE WEEK.

SUNDAY.

BREAKFAST.

Pork and beans, fish balls, Boston brown bread, wheaten grits, coffee.

DINNER.

Parker House soup, roast beef, sweet and white potatoes baked, macaroni, tomatoes, apple jelly, three cream pies, coffee.

TEA.

Sliced beef, cold ; brown and white bread, cup custards, canned peaches, cake—white mountain, tea.

MONDAY.

BREAKFAST.

Cold roast meat, fried sweet or white potatoes, breakfast rolls, hominy, fruit.

DINNER.

Dried bean or pea soup, roast veal, stewed tomatoes, white potatoes, macaroni, pie.

TEA.

Sally Lunn, stewed oysters, canned peaches, cream cake.

TUESDAY.

BREAKFAST.

Cold roast meat, broiled ; boiled eggs, baked potatoes, corn bread, oatmeal, coffee.

LUNCHEON.

Mutton chops, fried potatoes, sliced tomatoes, cream puffs, chocolate or tea.

TEA.

Egg plant, fried ; milk toast, peaches and cream, Mrs. E.'s gingerbread, coffee or tea.

WEDNESDAY.

BREAKFAST.

Shad, broiled ; potatoes, scalloped ; oatmeal and cream. French toast, graham gems, coffee.

DINNER.

Amber soup, roast chicken, potatoes—white, mashed ; potatoes—sweet, boiled ; beets, baked ; salad, pudding —apple tapioca ; pickled peaches, coffee or chocolate.

TEA.

Cold tongue, sliced bread—graham and white ; cake —jelly rolls ; coffee or tea.

THURSDAY.

BREAKFAST.

Chicken croquettes, potatoes—Saratoga; cracked wheat or grits, wheat bread, griddle cakes—buckwheat ; coffee.

LUNCHEON.

Fritters, sweet and white potatoes, green peas, pudding —peach, baked ; bread, coffee or cocoa.

TEA.

Beef ball, waffles, No. 1 ; quince preserves, buttered toast, tea.

FRIDAY.

BREAKFAST.

Chowder, eggs—poached ; potatoes—scalloped ; hominy, raised biscuit, coffee.

DINNER.

Sago soup, roast mutton ; baked sweet and white potatoes, cabbage salad, spinach, currant jelly, cherry pie, ice cream, coffee.

TEA.

Mutton, sliced ; soda biscuit, No. 1 ; canned peas, cake—Gussie's sponge ; coffee or tea.

SATURDAY.

BREAKFAST.

Beefsteak, broiled ; potatoes—stewed ; oatmeal, breakfast puffs, radishes, coffee.

LUNCHEON.

Oysters—panned ; potato scones, lettuce, apple-sauce, currant, raspberry or strawberry whisk, coffee.

TEA.

Dried beef omelette, raised biscuit, canned pineapple ; cake—jumbles, coffee or tea.

INDEX.

www.ingramcontent.com/pod-product-compliance
Lightning Source LLC
Chambersburg PA
CBHW020759020726
47495CB00008B/2506